The Feet of a Princess

A TRUE STORY OF HOPE, SURVIVAL AND TRANSFORMATION

BONITA B. WILLIAMS, J. D.

Christian Living
B O O K S
LARGO, MD

Christian Living Books, Inc.
P. O. Box 7584
Largo, MD 20792
christianlivingbooks.com

ISBN 978-1-56229-239-3

Scripture quotations are taken from the King James Version of the Bible.

Printed in the United States of America.

Library of Congress Cataloging-in-Publication Data

Names: Williams, Bonita B., 1950- author.
Title: The feet of a princess / Bonita B. Williams.
Description: Largo, MD : Christian Living Books, Inc., 2015.
Identifiers: LCCN 2015032455 | ISBN 9781562292393 (pbk. : alk. paper)
   ISBN 978-1-56229-244-7 (ebook)
Subjects: LCSH: Williams, Bonita B., 1950---Family. | African American
   women--Delaware--Wilmington--Biography. | African
   Americans--Delaware--Wilmington--Biography. | African Americans--Social
   life and customs--Delaware--Wilmington. | Wilmington (Del.)--Biography. |
   Wilmington (Del.)--History, Local.
Classification: LCC F174.W79 N39 2015 | DDC 305.48/89607307512--dc23 LC
record available at http://lccn.loc.gov/2015032455

Dedication

This book is dedicated to my nana, Addie Brown Foust; my paternal grandfather and grandmother, Lee and Sarah Byrd; my mother, Beily Paige Foust Byrd; my dad, Richard Byrd; Mrs. Hannah Johnson; Mr. and Mrs. James and Pearline White; Dr. Winder Porter and his wife, Gladys; and all of my neighbors and friends who lived up "on the hill" in Wilmington from the 1950s through the '90s. I thank you all for enriching my life, extending me kindness and providing me with a foundation from which I learned to navigate in this unpredictable world, so very different from the times when I visited in your homes – which I really miss. Most of you have gone on to glory and a well-deserved rest. I know we will see each other again, and then, we will have lots to share.

To Mrs. Bertha Allen
As Dorothy said in The Wizard of Oz, "There is no place like home." I hope my little book will help you revisit our home, Wilmington Delaware. It was a lovely little town full of good, solid people. I hope I have honored all of our ancestors and friends thru my story. May God bless and keep you. As a part of my reading audience we are now officially family.
Love n' hugs
Donita Williams

Table of Contents

Preface

THE LEGACY

It's all about the legacy. The word "legacy" means property or personal belongings gifted to a loved one by bequeath in a will. It is any item – material, intellectual, or spiritual – passed on to you by your ancestors or forbearers. Our legacy is that of the descendants of kings and queens who held on to their faith in a God they could not see. They traveled the Middle Passage from Africa to North America through a sea so littered with the bodies of our ancestors that sharks still travel this route because the taste and smell of their flesh and blood remain in these waters.

The members of my generation and I were the children of promise. We were the ones whose opportunities were built on the prayers, blood, and suffering of our ancestors for generations dating back to the 1500s on these shores. We walked across their bent backs, bowed heads, gnarled hands, and broken spirits through slavery, reconstruction, Jim Crow, and segregation into the land of milk and honey – that is, the land of integration and affirmative action.

On behalf of my generation, beloved, I have to apologize because we have failed you. My younger sisters and brothers, I want to ask you to forgive my generation and me. My daddy said the worst thing that could happen to the Negro was integration... and he was right because when we crossed over into the land of opportunity, we forgot our responsibility to pass the legacy forward. We marched out of church basements into the world. We were selfish and filled our lives with ourselves and our desires. We bought clothes, cars, more clothes, and maybe a house. When that didn't kill us, we bought alcohol and drugs, fornicated, and sinned against ourselves, our children, and our God.

Now, having awakened like a giant reeling with a hangover, the realization has hit us that we are coming to the end of our lives and we have failed to tell our children who they are, whose they are, where they come from, and where they need to go. As the Word says, "My people are destroyed for lack of knowledge" (Hosea 4:6).

As the children of promise, my generation has begun to awaken from its self-indulgence. We have begun to hear the voice of momma 'n them and the Good Shepherd, and none other shall we follow (John 10:1-5).

By the grace of God and the prayers of the righteous, our collective memories have kept the legacy – the baton that we must pass to our youth – intact. Our young people must be reminded:

The God we could not see kept us. He kept us alive, fed, and warm. He ordered our steps in His Word, and that is why we are here today. We must continue to humble ourselves and pray, and seek His face so that we may hear from Him what to do, how to do it, and when to do it. It is dependence on the living God that brings prosperity – not selling drugs, making music videos, or playing basketball.

We are the descendants of kings and queens, strong in mind, body, and soul. How else could we have survived the Middle Passage? Are you carrying yourself like the prince or princess that you are?

We must respect our elders and ancestors.

> Honour thy father and thy mother: that thy days may be long upon the land which the LORD thy God giveth thee. (Exodus 10:12)

Our youths are dying because they do not know this basic truth.

We survived because we worked hard, and we were proud of it. No job was too low to do to the best of our ability. Do not despise small beginnings (Zechariah 4:9-10). We must return to our former standards of excellence and committed, determined work ethic.

You must be educated. You must read. You must write. You must speak the King's English. Without these skills, you cannot function independently in this country.

Do not believe the lie. We are not what you see on television. We are not hip-jiggling, bumping, grinding, thugs, pimps, and lowlifes.

And if you don't believe the lie, don't support it. Don't buy CDs, movies, clothes, and products that do not support the real truth. If you aren't supporting the truth, you are helping to tell the lie.

We must love one another. We must love one another. We must love one another.

It's the struggle that keeps you strong. It builds the muscle of the mind, the spirit, and the body. Luxury creates weakness and leads to certain death when it is not directed to attain something greater than comforting oneself.

We must cease sacrificing our children for our own immediate need for income, comfort, and so on. Our children are the only future we have. Failure to focus on their good and to protect them from others who seek to benefit from their loss fosters murder, genocide, and even worse things. It is a sure end to our existence.

We must invest in our own – our men, our women, our children, our businesses. We have learned to distrust our own. We must reverse this curse. No other people on the planet behave in this manner. We cannot embrace affirmation from others until we affirm ourselves.

In closing, a couple of years ago, I had the pleasure of attending a conference held by Messianic Jews at Messiah College. T. D. Jakes was the keynote speaker, and the opportunity to hear him speak in an auditorium designed to hold five hundred people was too good to pass up. That night, he spoke passionately about the similarities between blacks and Jews. It was deeply moving and well received, so much so that they made T. D. Jakes a rabbi… on the spot. This is unheard of in Jewish tradition because it typically takes years of study and grooming to become a rabbi. At the close of the evening, the Holy Ghost fell, and the musicians sang and played songs quietly that spoke of the Jewish tradition and their oneness as a people. Quietly and slowly, the congregation members began to move among themselves as if on cue. They would stop every so often in front of one another, gazing deeply into one another's eyes, or they would pause and gently touch a cheek or embrace. There was a strong communal spirit shared during those moments that passed from breast to breast. Those present seemed to communicate among themselves wordlessly, "You were there; you were there with me at Joseph's death... at the Red Sea... during the Holocaust... at the Thirty Days' War... You were there, and you are one with me, and I with you."

We, too, need to stop and remember our commonality, our oneness, our unity. We need to pause and look into one another's eyes and remember we are one. Our destinies are inextricably intertwined for good or for bad. The choice is predicated upon a condition. If we stand together, in love and unity, with God, we shall prosper and be in good health. For it is at the point of unity that there is the commanded blessing.

> Behold, how good and how pleasant it is for brethren to dwell together in unity! Behold, how good and how pleasant it is for brethren to dwell together in unity. (Psalm 133:1)

Introduction
A HAPPIER TIME

Time has passed so quickly. It seems odd to me that I should be writing a memoir. Yesterday I was thirty years old with babies on my hip, a career to pursue, and a young husband to care for and keep up with. Today I am a gray-haired woman in my sixties with less time before me than behind.

I have so many stories to tell. Though I have too few people to share them with who would care to listen, I write these stories to share with you that there was a better, happier time in Wilmington, Delaware, when people were kind and happy. Life was much gentler, and love was available for those of us desiring to reach out for it. Then, we were colored people and Negroes living and working in fairly close communities. We respected our elders, treated our neighbors like family, worked hard, and attended school. Most importantly, we were taught that nothing was as important as serving God and getting an education because Jesus and an education were the only things that could never be taken away from you. That was a mantra repeated by about any significant elder with whom one interacted. If you were female, you knew the worst thing that could ever happen to you was for you to become pregnant out of wedlock. After all, opportunity and a better way of life depended upon your chastity, along with an education and Jesus. Of course, racism existed in the greater community, but within the neighborhood on the hill in Wilmington where I was blessed to live, we lived, loved, had fun, and thrived.

In fact, my fondest childhood memories center around my home there, at 301 North Cleveland Avenue. It was a beautiful two-story white stucco home built by my nana, Addie Brown Foust, in the 1940s as a shelter and home for her and her daughter, Beily Paige Foust. At the top of an incline close to the western boundary of the city, several beautiful single-family dwellings formed the beginnings of a middle-class Negro neighborhood. Cleveland Avenue, which ran perpendicular to the numeric streets, marked the end of the city transportation system. Mrs. Bernice Stubbs, the first Negro Realtor in Delaware, had helped several families purchase land and build homes in the vicinity, which previously had been the location of an old stone quarry. The quarry had been filled in years earlier, and the vacant land had become arable and suitable for residential facilities. Mrs. Stubbs seized the opportunity and began to quietly locate her clients in clean, safe, sanitary housing of an upscale style, location, and quality befitting their "up-and-coming" status as the burgeoning Negro middle class developing post-World War II in northern New Castle County, Delaware. Through Stubbs Realty, Bernice Stubbs began to shape a new community comprised of professionals and people of quality. The homes and building lots "on the hill" were made available to professionals and people of stature in the community that she carefully identified and screened.

As a resident of the community herself, Mrs. Stubbs had a vested interest in the composition of the neighborhood. The more established, traditional housing opportunities on the East Side of Wilmington and in Millside, a former army barracks turned low-income housing for Negroes in suburban New Castle County, were becoming overly crowded. Returning veterans and younger professionals were more demanding and wanted their families out of center city. "On the hill," as it came to be known, was the perfect answer. White working-class folks – police officers and firemen – already lived in the town houses that stretched north to south along the numbered streets, but the streets with names – Cleveland, Ogle, and so on – were wide-open territory and presented an opportunity for a hustling businesswoman such as Bernice Stubbs.

Addie Brown Foust was one of Mrs. Stubbs' first clients. Having pinched and scrupulously saved every nickel and dime of her salary possible, Addie purchased the plot at the corner of Third Street and Cleveland Avenue. Beautifully, but modestly, appointed, 301 offered amenities similar to those of the homes Addie had worked in as a cook her entire life. It provided a shelter and a home for Beily and, later, Beily's husband, Richard, and their children. It offered a setting in which to teach her grandchildren the ways and the manners of educated people and most of all a place to build family and promote legacy. Addie accomplished more than she would ever know in the purchase of that lovely house. If I close my eyes and let my mind drift, I can almost hear my nana and momma in the kitchen now...

Allow me to take you there. It is my hope that the vignettes in the following chapters will give a younger generation a glimpse of what it was like to grow up during the 1950s in a black middle-class community in Wilmington. We have lost so much, and I am afraid we will never recapture the innocence, the security, and the unity of that time. I am sure my mentors felt much the same way as they pushed through the '60s and '70s into the '90s. In contrast to the sages of our past, my question is not the same as Marvin Gaye's: "What's going on?" Mine is more along the lines of Francis Schaeffer's: "Where, oh where are we headed, my people? And having arrived in this space and time that we are now in, how should we then live?"

Chapter 1

THE WARMEST WELCOME

Evening had settled quietly around the homes on the hill in the West Side of Wilmington. A car motor idled in front of the small white stucco home at Third Street and Cleveland Avenue. First, one door opened and shut, and then a second door opened. A light brown, softly rounded woman in a heavy brown coat, a dark striped skirt, and a hat with a woolen scarf tied over it leaned out of the car, handing trays wrapped in waxed paper and aluminum foil to an older white man dressed in a dark coat and hat. The man ascended three steps from the sidewalk, crossed the landing at the top with two short, clipped steps, made one quick step up to the door, and rang the bell. A beautiful young woman in her early thirties opened the door.

"Hello, Mr. Kowalski. Momma with you?"

"Yes," he smiled. "And here are some of the goodies."

Beily opened the door to the sunporch and received the trays he handed her, and then she placed them on any flat surface available. He made three more trips before she heard her mother's voice, "Thank you, Joseph. I'll see you tomorrow evening." Shortly thereafter, Beily could hear her mother's slower, heavier ascent.

"Hello, Momma," she said.

"Hello, 'Ginger,'" her mother replied. "Beily, you will catch your death out here; I'll bring these things in."

Upstairs in her bedroom, Bonnie could hear the quiet commotion. A visitor at this time of night could only mean one thing: Nana was home! Nana's visit was better than anything in the world – better than

Christmas, birthday parties, or running through the sprinkler! Nana meant hot rolls, pound cake with chocolate icing, tea parties, and lots 'n lots of hugs and kisses. Bonnie pushed her strong little four-year-old body over the crib siding and landed with a soft thud beside the bed. Her sister, named Beily Paige after their mother, slept quietly in the crib, kitty-corner next to her. Bonnie had nicknamed her "Boo Boo" because "Beily" was too hard to pronounce. Listening carefully to her sister's breathing, Bonnie detected a barely audible wheeze, the sound that always made the furrow between her mommy's eyes. It wasn't a bad sound tonight, though. Bonnie eased quietly toward the door.

It was the early 1950s, and people turned their heat down and wore flannel pajamas and socks to stay warm. Never feeling comfortable with socks on while under the covers, Bonnie always squiggled her feet out of the socks. Even so, the house was cold, and she could see little puffs of frosty air coming out of her mouth in the moonlight. She crept past the door to her room and stood briefly outside of her parents' room to the left. The baby's crib was in there. Richard Lee was the only boy. He was round with a round head and big round eyes. He seemed to babble, holler, and eat all the time, but he was asleep then, quiet and cute. *That's probably why they kept him around,* she mused.

From there, Bonnie quietly descended the stairs into the living room, crossed into the dining room, and stood at the entry to the kitchen, waiting to be discovered. It didn't take long.

"Baby, sweet baby," Nana said, turning to face her.

"Nana! Nana! Nana!" Bonnie cried joyfully, running to squeeze her grandmother around her knees, feeling the outside cold and her warm, pudgy body, and smelling the wonderful elixir of yeast and baking bread.

Beily knelt down, looking into her daughter's eyes, and said firmly, but smiling, "Bonnie Aileen, you are supposed to be in bed." Bonnie was a precocious little girl who sounded a lot older than she was. Standing there with her three braids askew like an off-centered TV antenna, her flannel pajamas, her ever-present plaid skirt, and bare feet, it was clear that this little person had overheard her nana was coming home today, and she had made plans to await her arrival.

"Can't I have just one roll with jelly before I go to bed?" she wheedled. Before Beily could answer, Nana replied, "Of course you can." Quickly, Nana reached for one of the baskets she'd brought with her. She folded back a linen towel to reveal a basket filled with gently browned yeast rolls laid out row after row like marching soldiers in a parade. While the rolls were still warm from the oven, Nana took a teaspoon of grape jelly from the counter and inserted it into the middle of a roll, where it joined a pat of melted butter.

She wrapped the warm, oozing concoction in a napkin and handed it to Bonnie. "C'mon, sit on my lap," Beily said. "The floor is cold."

Bonnie sat happily on her mother's lap, carefully taking tiny bites to prolong her presence with the two pillars of her world. Seeing them together, smiling and chatting in the glow of the kitchen, and having them all to herself was a wonderful, rare moment. Who knew when it would happen again?

"Okay, it's bedtime, little girl," Beily announced.

"Nana, you coming too?" Bonnie asked.

"As soon as I get this food put away. Night-night, now."

Bonnie walked over to her mom, hugged her around the neck, and kissed her cheek, leaving a smudge of butter and jelly. She turned to Nana and kissed both cheeks, leaving the same residue.

"Nighty-night," she said, quickly going up the steps. She climbed up the side of the crib and plopped on top of the mattress; then she pulled the covers up quickly. *Tomorrow will be a great day*, she thought, and yawned. *Nana is home!* She yawned again and quickly drifted off to sleep.

Sometime in the middle of the night, Bonnie awoke. Across the room, at the far wall, was the outline of a body under the covers in the twin bed. Nana! she thought. Bonnie clambered out of the bed and dropped gently on the floor. She walked over to the bed and stood eye level, watching her grandmother sleep. "Oh! Baby!" Nana exclaimed, her eyes opening quickly, suddenly aware she was being watched. "Come in here; you'll catch your death." Nana moved further back along the mattress, closer to the wall, allowing space for Bonnie to enter. Bonnie crawled into the bed and rolled over into the warmth of Nana's body. The last parts of her to reach Nana were her ice-cold feet. "Whew!" Nana jumped, "Turn around, and let me warm those feet of yours." Nana took each foot in her hands and rubbed it softly, but vigorously. "They are sweet little feet... the feet of a princess. Warm now?" she asked. "Mmm hmm," Bonnie sighed, and she quickly fell asleep in her nana's arms.

THERE'S NO PLACE LIKE HOME

Addie Brown Foust was a determined, purposed woman. Born in Reidsville, North Carolina, on April 10, 1898, on a Cherokee Indian reservation, Addie had learned the craft, skill, and art of cooking good food at an early age. In her late teens, she met Arthur Foust, a much older man working as a butler in the home of a wealthy, white family.

It was well known that Arthur, nicknamed "OW," or "Off White," was the offspring of the head of the white Foust family and one of the household's black employees. So much racial mixture had occurred in that particular section of Greensboro, North Carolina, that it was said of a major corridor in the city that one side was occupied by the white Fousts, and the other side, by the black Fousts. It was one of the oddities of life resulting from the South's peculiar institutions: slavery, miscegenation, and segregation. Clearly, someone (or more than one) had jumped the fence of race, and more than once.

Arthur was jolly, dashing, and handsome with an unfortunate tendency to drink too much alcohol. Far too often, he would get drunk on his way home and end up calling out in the late-night hour, "Addie! C'ain't you help me?" Addie faithfully helped him until one day his kidneys and liver failed him. She buried him with her love and took their daughter, Beily, and went north, leaving behind her hurt and pain and a land that offered no opportunity for her or her daughter. *Beily had to have better, had to do better*, she thought. The North, they said, offered that better chance – a better education, better working conditions, and a chance to pull yourself up to a better life.

Addie pressed north with her little girl, their bags, and her mother, Rebecca Brown's big iron pot. She landed in Concordville, Pennsylvania, and found employment with the Swain family. They had been the first family to cultivate mushrooms as a crop in the United States. The job permitted her to keep Beily with her, too, which was a rarity during those times. Things were going well until one day, one of the Swain boys, who was deaf with a speech impediment resulting from a cleft palate, referred to Beily as a "Ba' faced injun gal."

When Addie overheard him referring to her daughter with that terminology, it was just a bit too reminiscent of the South she had so recently left. So, she and Beily packed up, and soon Addie found a home for the two of them. By this time, Addie had made a few friends among the residents of the small Negro community in Kennett Square, Pennsylvania. She began to attend the local Methodist church and establish friendships. Biggie Hunt, a relocated butler, also from North Carolina, was working for the Wise family of Wilmington. Ruth Brown, a local Pennsylvanian who had grown up in the area, became a valued and trusted friend. Biggie was good and kind. He was protective and secure and showed Addie the idiosyncrasies of the wealthy, northern white families they both served.

During this time, Addie became seriously ill and required a hysterectomy and a long convalescence. This occurred during the 1930s, during the Depression, when there was no health insurance, only cash, and no such thing as disability pay. Despite this, Addie, always thrifty, had managed to save enough money for the operation. Ruth had offered her a place to stay during her recuperation, but how could she care for Beily? Suppose she didn't survive the operation or was unable to return to work, to stand on her feet and cook and clean up eighteen to twenty hours a day? Addie worried and prayed: "Lord, I'm here in a foreign land. Help me to live and raise my daughter." Not one to give in to emotion, Addie slowly came up with a plan. Beily would have to find shelter and work. Only God would know where Beily should be, and Addie trusted Him to find the perfect place for her Beily. Addie explained their lot slowly and deliberately to Beily. The tearful little ten-year-old clung to her mother and cried until her face was swollen and red, but Addie was firm and unemotional. The world was a hard, cruel place for colored people and especially for colored female children. Beily would have to learn now to make decisions in a calm, unemotional state and to stand independently alone. That was life for a colored girl in the 1930s and, as far as Addie knew, the foreseeable future.

Beily went on a job hunt with guidance from her mother. Painfully and with many tears, Beily walked up and down the streets of Kennett Square seeking a position and shelter. She'd lost her father and relocated to a colder version of Greensboro, and now she was possibly losing her mother, too.

But God showed up, just as Addie had prayed that He would. Shortly thereafter, Beily went to live with Miss Brauna Apple and her sister, two elderly Quaker ladies in need of a companion. Beily had safe, decent, clean housing among solidly upper-middle class, God-fearing people who treated Negroes fairly. As former schoolteachers, the Apple sisters would be able to teach Beily how to conduct herself among learned people, earn a living, and be trained in the etiquette of a lady. Beily lived with them through her graduation from Kennett High School, in 1941. She learned to read, sew, draw, and occupy her quiet time usefully. On Sundays, she was able to visit her mother during her convalescence at Mrs. Brown's home. Addie survived the operation and found work once again in the kitchen of wealthy whites in the Kennett Square area. Under the guidance of the Apple sisters and Addie's careful eye, Beily had been given the choice of becoming a schoolteacher or a nurse. Beily chose nursing and entered Provident Hospital in Baltimore, Maryland. Addie had preferred a school in Boston. Her rationale: Always press north. But "Ginger," as Beily's nickname became, wanted to have greater opportunities to form friendships among her own people. Addie's youngest sister, Ethel, lived in Washington, D.C. and was married to a handsome, loving man named Monte. Aunt Ethel worked for the Department of Defense, and Uncle Monte was an auto mechanic who played golf. Beily wanted that type of life, too.

Addie realized that she had to establish a home for her and her daughter. Beily had to have a place of her own to come home to. Having lost her entire savings in bank accounts during the Depression, Addie had managed to save enough money from her paltry salary of twenty-five dollars a month to buy a home. After Addie explored the idea of moving to Philadelphia, Beily exclaimed, "Momma, if you keep on pushing north, we're going to end up in Canada! How about Wilmington?"

Wilmington it was. Addie found a small plot of land on the West Side of Wilmington, where an old stone quarry used to be. She bought the land and had a house built on it for five thousand dollars. It was a beautiful, white stucco home with red trim, a sunporch across the front, a living room with a wood-burning fireplace, a formal dining room, an eat-in kitchen, three bedrooms, and a bath on the second floor, as well as an attached, one-car garage. Dubbed "the Little Acre," 301 North Cleveland Avenue became the homestead for Addie and Beily, and later Beily; her husband, Richard; and their three children.

Chapter 3

REASON FOR CELEBRATION

Beily graduated as a registered nurse from Provident Hospital and came home to Wilmington. Through the intervention of Addie's employer, Beily Paige Foust became the first Negro visiting nurse in Delaware. Her assignments were the population of the East Side of Wilmington, South Wilmington, and Millside, the former army barracks turned housing for dislocated Negroes migrating from the South seeking low-cost housing and relief from urban redlining policies. In her starched white uniform, nursing cap, and stylish navy wool cape lined with red, she cut quite a dashing figure. Beily had grown to become a beautiful young lady. Fair-skinned with long, reddish-brown hair that reached her shoulders, a pompadour, full lips, and an aquiline nose; she was lovely. Her kind, efficient care drew a lot of attention and respect. Negro registered nurses were a new thing in Wilmington, which was as southern as Greensboro. The landed gentry just managed the folks a bit differently.

While Beily completed her education at Provident Hospital in Baltimore, Maryland, World War II was raging. The nursing program was grueling, and classmates, often unkind. Theft was de rigueur, and Negro-on-Negro discrimination was common among students and faculty alike. Light skin and long hair translated into strangers pulling your hair up at the back of your neck to see if you had a kinky nape. It also meant extra cleaning assignments on the ward. It didn't matter to Beily. Throw what they may her way; she was determined to graduate... and she did.

Sometime during the period of high school, nursing school,

9

graduation as a registered nurse, and the end of World War II, Beily met Richard Byrd. Richard was of medium height and had pecan brown skin, sparkling white teeth, and dark brown hair eased into curls with Murray's hair pomade. He, too, was of southern lineage, hailing from Havana (pronounced Hayvanna), Florida, an old plantation on the panhandle of the state.

Richard's father, Lee, and *his* father, known as "Feddoe," raised and tended cattle. Feddoe was a huge man, around six feet eight inches tall and three hundred pounds. Lee, the eldest son, was much slighter in build, often referred to as the runt of the family. But what Lee lacked in height and girth he made up for in good looks. Even in his seventies and later, Lee was a good-looking man. He had a complexion like coffee with lots of cream in it, and soft, wavy, snow-white hair. Like many black men who migrated north in 1928, there was a whispered story about a fight with a white man who threatened his wife, Sarah. The family consisting of Lee; Sarah; Airee D., later known as "Richard"; and his brother, Rokie, also known as "Roosevelt," joined the huge numbers of Negroes migrating north in 1928. What Lee's real last name was in Florida is still in dispute, but when he arrived in Claymont, Delaware, it was Lee Byrd, and that is what it remained.

Sarah Robinson Byrd was a small, bony, fragile, dark brown woman with tiny, bead-like eyes that darted, furtively, whenever they were open. She wore her hair short and combed straight into a bob with bangs. On most occasions, she wore a black net over her hair to keep it in place. She spoke very little, but chuckled a small nervous sound in response to most questions. She and Lee had married when she was thirteen and he was seventeen. He had rescued Sarah from her mother, Coote, a full-blooded Seminole Indian who was as cruel as she was beautiful. Lee and Sarah remained as tight as a skein of yarn all of their lives, with a language and cadence all their own, impenetrable to the coldness of northern weather or the people who lived there. They wrapped their sons into that network of love, trying their best to insulate and protect their sons from the cold and cruelty that only the North could offer a former Southerner.

The move north was difficult for the family. Lee occasionally got drunk. He would sit on the porch in a wool coat, smoking a Camel cigarette and sipping on Gordon's gin. "Sarah, I wants to go home. It's cold up here, and the peoples is mean." Sarah and the boys would put him to bed, and Lee would get up every morning, Monday through Friday, and walk from Hickman Row over the hill, carrying his lunch pail and thermos, to work to support his family at Worth Steel for twelve-plus hours a day.

Sarah struggled in her adjustment to the North, too. Quiet and withdrawn, she anesthetized herself from the cold and separation from kin and kind with gin, snuff, and Pepsi. Never a person of energy or strength, Sarah did day work for the Cauffiel family, which lived on the Philadelphia Pike, cooking and cleaning. Eventually, her sister Lula and her niece, Daisy Price, found their way to Hickman Row, bringing with them the warmth and comfort that only family blood can bring.

Richard was a product of his background. Born in Havana in 1918 amongst family and friends and the warmth and predictability of life on a cattle ranch, Richard was used to running barefoot in the dust, skipping stones in the stream, and riding in the wagon with his dad and granddad Feddoe. Feddoe was the foreman of the ranch, and that title brought with it some degree of status and perquisites. While Feddoe had a commanding physical presence and strength, he was also a smart man. He managed the Havana plantation, and what he said was done. Things were as secure and predictable as they could be for a colored family in the early 1900s.

However, everything changed in 1923 with the Depression. Work on the plantation had dried up. Lee and Sarah had babies to feed, and opportunities at home were not easy to come by. Sarah was being threatened by outside forces beyond Lee's control. That left only one option: to move north, where it was rumored there was work. Like many other colored families of the times, the Byrds packed up and left under the protection of night. In that manner, no one had to explain to the plantation owner or the authorities what had happened or why he or she had left. The Byrds became part of the Great Migration of colored folks moving north, seeking a better way of life for themselves and their children.

Up north, it was cold, and there was no land and space to run and play in like back home. People were mean and conniving. Lee, Sarah, and their two sons found their way to Hickman Row. The difference in the weather, landscape, people's attitude, and employment was challenging and difficult, but manageable. Unlike any other area in Delaware, Worth Steel in Claymont offered its Negro employees safe, decent housing and a school nearby for the children. These amenities were immensely important to Negro families striving for better opportunities for their offspring. Claymont was also a good place to get lost in if you were concerned that "the law" of the state of your former, southern residence may be hunting for you.

There, language became the surprising and overwhelming barrier the family faced. The instant derogatory reaction to their soft southern accent and drawl would elicit ridicule, hurt, stings, and burns that affected the speech patterns of generations yet unborn. As the first child in the family to interact with the education system in Claymont, Richard experienced the brunt of the name-calling and humiliation.

On his first day of school, when the teacher, Pauline Dyson, asked his name, he replied "Airee, Airee D." Deciding that his name was unsuitable, she renamed him Richard. His brother, Rokie, became Roosevelt. And that was that. Ms. Dyson, with her short, thick, fireplug-shaped body and gleaming silver hair braided and wrapped in a bun, ran the State Line School like Attila the Hun. With a master's in education from Columbia University, Pauline was determined to whip the uneducated, poor, colored Southerners into Du Bois' Talented Tenth or kill them in the attempt. From a one-room segregated school, housing prekindergarten through eighth grade, she pounded into them, mentally and physically, every bit of education, music, and art that a colored child could access in the Claymont public school system from 1918 to 1957.

Soon, Richard managed to erase every trace of his southern accent and dialect from his spoken language. His ability to "speak the King's English" enabled him to negotiate the larger world on behalf of his family. The windows of Richard's world were extended by his beautiful, tenor singing voice and his intellect. Ms. Dyson showcased his talents traveling throughout the Mid-Atlantic region, with Richard competing in various and sundry talent shows. He competed to such an extent and with such frequency that he complained his throat hurt. As soon as he was able to escape the voice competitions, he ceased to sing.

Richard was a man of exceptional intelligence. He graduated from Howard High School at sixteen and spent a year at Delaware State College. Not challenged sufficiently, he transferred to Cheney State University, where he completed his sophomore year. Then World War II happened. The war changed everything, quickly and suddenly. Richard and Roosevelt were drafted. Richard was sent to the European front, and Roosevelt, to Africa. Like many families on Hickman Row, Lee and Sarah watched their children go to war. The boys left for foreign shores, uncertain as to what to expect, and their parents prayed for their safe and quick return.

Richard was trained at Fort Brevard and then sent to London. He enjoyed London, its people, its weather, and its history. For the first time in his life, Richard experienced freedom. He could go where he wanted, drink water where he wanted, and eat where he wanted, and no one stopped him because he was colored. Not even the "chollies" (rhymes with *jollies*, translated "Charlies") – white folks from America – could restrict him on the basis of his color in London. Richard was a staff sergeant. He was a free man, and he functioned like one, with no limits.

Throughout his entire war experience, Richard researched the law to try to find a legal way out of his service. White folks had no problem coming up with ways for you to die in America; they just had real problems allowing you to live. Always handsome and easy with women, Richard was pursued by many women in London tired of the war, tired of a lack of male presence and company. Soon, he found his way to the Palladium Ballroom with some of his buddies, where he would spend many evenings dancing away fears, anxiety, and the excitement of being free in a different country and culture. After spending about two years in London, he relocated to France, where he was promoted to staff sergeant. He finished the bulk of the war in France, earning a Victory Medal for his leadership in the demolition squads.

War changes people, and Richard was no exception. He was angry that he was returning to a country that did not recognize or respect his manhood. Neither did America recognize his fighting to maintain freedom for his country when it failed to grant freedom to him and his fellow "Tan Yanks on the Front." He became deeply cynical about this country, white folks in general, and the Germans and Japanese, in particular. He viewed most people skeptically and kept nearly everyone at arm's length, rarely reaching out for comfort in a way that could be understood.

One person Richard did reach out to was Beily, and she responded with naiveté and kindness. Lonely and alone much of her life, insular for many of the same reasons, Beily bonded with Richard. Each of them searched for a security he or she had not engaged as children, a security that had fallen apart and was unable to be reconstructed, always being among, but not of, others. They forged an alliance and friendship that blossomed into a fragile love. She was seeking a husband, stability, a home, and children. He was craving for a woman, completeness, a home, and children. Finding enough of what they sought, they married. As many young and in love, they shared just enough truth to attract, but not enough to reveal... both titillating and fatal.

Chapter 4

THE GOOD LIFE

Bonnie turned over, expecting to roll against the warmth of her grandmother, as she slowly eased her mind into consciousness. No such luck. Instead, the sheets were cool against her back, and as her hand began to reach out, gingerly in an upward-moving arch, it was obvious Nana had gotten up. Slowly, the smell of hot yeast bread and bacon wafted toward her. She inhaled deeply, sat up, and rubbed her eyes open. She turned on her side and pushed onto the floor. In her crib, Boo also was sitting up, smiling and ready to get busy. "C'mon, Boo. Nana's here," Bonnie said. "But first we gotta go." After a quick stop in the bathroom with half-zipped sleepers, the girls slid down the carpeted steps on their stomachs. It was a technique they'd perfected over time, learning to angle their feet, head, and elbows just so to permit the area from the chest to the knee to flatten out and slide perfectly over the steps straight from the second to the first floor nonstop without a bruise. Just as they hit the bottom with a thud and a giggle, they heard a wail and a whimper. "Mom, it's Skipper," Bonnie said as she and Boo bounded around the corner, then through the living room and into the kitchen.

"Good morning, girls," Beily said, leaning down. "Morning, Mommy!" they squealed. Boo hugged Beily's leg, and Bonnie hugged around Boo and kissed her momma. Nana, who was facing the stove, said, "Good morning, babies" as the girls turned toward her and hugged her knees. "I was just getting some toast ready for you." "Momma, I'm going to get the baby ready; I'll be right back," Beily said. The girls scrabbled onto the chairs next to their mini kitchen table. A half slice of toast cut into a diamond, with bubbly butter, fresh from the broiler, a crisp half slice of bacon, and a tablespoon of scrambled eggs were on each of the two saucers. Using their child-sized cutlery, Bonnie and Boo ate while they watched the kitchen comings and goings. From the radio, they heard Doris Day sing "How Much Is That Doggie in the Window," and the girls sang the chorus in between bites. Beily reappeared with Skipper, the round, brown bomber, who reached with his chubby fist for his bottle and his mommy.

"And where is Richard?" Nana was always careful in the pronunciation of consonants; D's, T's, and R's were of particular concern. It was the fight against the lazy tongue, and she, mom, and dad were vigilant in the fight.

"He's in Claymont, working on the house," Beily replied. "Mmmm," Nana said.

Richard had been building the house for most of their married life. First, he built a white, stucco, Cape Cod cottage for his parents and brother. Then, next to that property, he built a home for his wife and children. He'd used his savings, as well as Beily's, some of Nana's, and his veterans benefits to build a state-of-the-art rancher for his family in Claymont. Every morning, he worked on the rancher before he went to work at the steel mill. Also, he worked on the house after work and all weekend to finish it. The beautiful, red brick house was a grand sight to behold, with picture windows, a covered porch and patio, a master suite, three bedrooms, a living room, a dining room, an eat-in kitchen, and a two-car garage. It was a slice of heaven for a Negro family in the 1950s and well worth the wait.

Nevertheless, the separation between Beily and Richard as the home was being built did bring its stresses. While Richard visited 301 sporadically, he preferred to stay in Claymont with his parents so he could get to and from the steel mill easily. Beily stayed at her mother's home with the children, getting assistance from a day nanny, Mattie, who oversaw Bonnie, Boo, and Skip while she went to work for the Visiting Nurse Association. It was an uneasy living arrangement, but the goal – the red rancher – made it bearable for both parties. In the interim, everybody stepped carefully around Richard's absence, even the children. When Daddy came home, Bonnie had gotten into the habit of crawling into Beily and Richard's bedroom and lying under the bed just to hear them sleeping together. Skip must have sensed something, too, because he would holler until Richard picked him up and put him on his chest in bed. Boo would wake up crying, and Beily would put her in the bed, too. Then Richard would discover Bonnie under the bed and return her to her bedroom. Eventually, Richard would get up and sleep in the bedroom at the far end of the house, on top of the garage. Maybe it was the "musical beds" at night or his reluctance to sleep in his mother-in-law's home, but Richard was never comfortable at 301, and they all knew it.

"Girls, let's get washed up and dressed," Beily said, putting Skipper on her hip and guiding the girls toward the stairs.

"We're going to have a tea party, so come back quick," Nana called up the stairs after them.

Boo and Bonnie jumped up and down, clapping their hands gleefully. The girls snatched off their pj's and quickly donned their undies, sweaters, and overalls. They splashed water on their faces and hands and scrambled into shoes. They reappeared in the kitchen looking more like the Little Rascals than two young ladies preparing for a tea party.

Nana sat the girls at their table with a small mound of yeast dough in front of them. "Now pat the dough gently and get it ready for the goodies," she said. Obediently, the girls flattened the dough with their chubby, baby hands. "Sticky," said Boo, peering at her hands, flecked with yeast dough. "You need flour, baby," said Nana, and she sprinkled just enough flour on Boo's hand to eliminate the stickiness.

"That's it – pat, pat, pat," Nana said softly. "Bea-u-tee-ful," she said to Bonnie with a smile. She turned away to the counter, to a cinnamon-butter-nutmeg mixture with some raisins, and returned to the girls' table just long enough to deposit it in the center of their mound of dough. "Now, roll the edges up, girls, for the cinnamon buns." Each girl rolled her bun together in her own fashion. Neither had the softly rounded uniformity of the buns in Nana's pan, but there was promise that with continued repetition, these little sous chefs might become great bakers, too.

Next, the girls watched as Nana unloaded the oven's bounty, rows of yeast rolls. Then she reloaded the oven with cinnamon buns and quickly put softened butter on the tops of the rolls that had just come out of the oven. She selected one roll, broke it in half, and placed half in front of each girl. As they nibbled the roll, Nana moved quietly among her pots on the stove. Her movements were a bit stiff-legged due to arthritis, but she stirred her pots with the grace of a conductor before a philharmonic.

Addie Foust could really cook. Raised on an Indian reservation in Reidsville, North Carolina, she had been taken in by two Quaker missionaries and taught the culinary arts. It was a skill that served her well, enabling her to raise her daughter, send her to nursing school, and build her home. Now Addie was investing what she had learned in that area into her grandchildren, and teach them well she did.

"Time to polish the silver and set the table," Nana said. To Nana, silver had great significance. It represented wealth, stability, dignity, and culture, as of the families she'd served all her life. Silver told a story. It was collected over many generations, passed down through the family, and conveyed achievement, beauty, and proper etiquette. It all began with polishing the silver.

Nana spread the kitchen table with newspaper and brought out old, clean white diapers cut into squares for rags and a large jar of gray silver polish. One end of the kitchen table was stacked with grayish-blue, felt bags containing the precious silver. Carefully, she would remove a piece from a bag and begin to dab the silver polish on the rag. Gently, she would work the polish over the silver, lifting off the drab, gray tarnish and revealing the sparkling silver underneath. It was like magic. Nana would give Boo and Bonnie pieces of silver cutlery and their own cloths to work with. Boo soon grew tired. After all, this was work, and she was more interested in finding Mommy than working. She trailed off, leaving her fork still gloppy with polish. Bonnie worked away at the cutlery, wiping and polishing until five forks, spoons, and knives were gleaming. Nana polished the entire tea set – the tray, coffee pot, teapot, sugar bowl, creamer, and sugar tongs.

After that, Nana smoothed a clean, white damask tablecloth over the dining room table and eased the polished tea set onto the corner. She stood back to admire her handiwork as it gleamed in the sunlight. Wiping her hands on her apron, she looked down at Bonnie, standing beside her. Nana's hand eased Bonnie's braids into place. "I think we can set the table now, baby," she said. "Get the china and the linen napkins."

"The napkins with the 'B' on them?" Bonnie asked.

"Yes, baby." Nana reached into the china closet and selected the luncheon plates, bread plates, cups, and saucers, while Bonnie opened the bottom drawers, pulling out linen napkins that Nana had hand-embroidered. "You set the table, Bonnie." Carefully, Bonnie set five places: forks on the left, spoons and knives on the right with the curve of the knife turned toward the plate in the center. Then, she placed the luncheon plates in the center of each set of cutlery. Last, but not least, she placed a napkin to the left of the fork, and the cup and saucer to the right of the knife at each setting. "Don't forget the doilies, Bonnie," Nana said. "Okeydokey," Bonnie replied. She found a packet of saucer-sized doilies in the china cabinet, carefully pulled them apart, and placed one doily under each saucer. "Look, Nana!" she exclaimed. Nana walked into the dining room to observe. "It is very elegant, Bonnie. Well done. I am really going to enjoy your tea party."

"I'm going to put my skirt on, Nana. I want to be pretty for the party." Bonnie bounced happily up the stairs to put on her favorite, plaid skirt. "Ginger, it's time for lunch, so bring the children," Nana called upstairs.

Beily and the children descended the stairs with much clambering and noise. She put Skipper down to walk, and the girls skipped into the dining room and climbed onto the chairs. Beily and Addie sat at either end of the table. "Momma, everything smells sooo good," Beily said. Nana brought in roast beef with gravy, baby peas with tiny white onions, stewed tomatoes, twice-baked potatoes, and hot rolls. She set out large glasses with sweet iced tea steeped with oranges and cloves for herself and Beily, and demitasse cups with milk for the children. "Bonnie, please say grace," Beily said. "Thank you for the birds that sing. Thank you for the food we eat. Thank you, God, for everything. Ahh-men." After the blessing, Addie served everyone's plate; Beily and Skipper shared one.

Then, the front door opened, and a heavy foot crossed the sunporch into the living room. "Richard! You're home!" Beily said, rising to embrace her husband. "Hello, Beily," Richard said, returning his wife's embrace a bit stiffly. Hugs were always difficult for Richard, it seemed. "Look at that fat, little boy," he said, chucking Skipper under the chin and smiling at his drooling namesake as he reached to hold the little boy. "Hi, Daddy," Bonnie said. Boo sucked her finger and went over to hug her daddy's knee. "You're just in time for lunch!" Nana said. "Hi, Nana," he replied as Addie rose to fix him a plate.

It was life in perfection. All of her significant others were in one place at the same time. They had good food, good times, good love and, as with all good things, it had to end. Richard, Beily, Boo, and Skipper returned to the living room, tummies tight, happy to be together after a long week apart. Bonnie followed Nana from the dining room to the kitchen as Nana cleaned up and put away the food. Being on the clean-up crew had real advantages, including running your fingers around the base of the cake to get a big scoop of chocolate icing without getting caught. But the best part was just being close to Nana, watching her, listening to her hum, watching her comb her hair, and smelling her special hot rolls and jelly.

All too soon, the sun had lowered in the sky, and Nana was beginning to put on her layers to leave: the sweaters, the wool skirt, the hat, the scarf. The doorbell rang. "It's Joseph, Momma," said Beily. "Hi, Mr. Kowalski." Bonnie overheard her mother say, "She'll be right out." The door to the sunporch was cracked, and the cold winter air cut into the living room like a knife. "Let me help you down the steps," Richard said. Boo started to cry. Big tears rolled down her cheeks like little diamonds. Then Skipper started to whimper. Bonnie ran to Nana and hugged her knees. "Don't go, Nana. Don't go. Please don't go," Bonnie pleaded.

"But if I don't go, we can't have the tea party. I'll be back real soon, I promise." She kissed Bonnie's cheeks, and patted Boo's head and Skipper's cheek. "Stay sweet; I love you." She turned, and Richard took her arm, then walked her down the steps and across the sidewalk to the car. He shut the door firmly and waved good-bye as the car turned right and drove into the night.

Chapter 5

SATURDAYS ON MARKET STREET

For Beily and the children, Saturdays were always full of activity. The girls studied ballet and tap dance at the Walnut Street YMCA, which was the social and cultural hub for the Negro population in Wilmington. Prior to desegregation, the Walnut Street "Y," as it was known to locals, provided lodging for travelers, good food, a library, a swimming pool, a ballroom-cum-theater, and meeting rooms of all shapes and sizes. The Y was a combination recreational-cultural-community center for the Negro population, and at one time or another, the leadership and ne'er-do-wells all rubbed elbows at the lunch counter.

On Saturday morning, from nine to twelve, Madame France, a displaced Frenchwoman, taught classical ballet classes to young, Negro girls seeking to develop poise and carriage. Patiently, Madame took her students, ages two through seventeen, through their basic positions at the barre to the rhythm of a pianist playing Chopin or Schubert. "Plié... Relevé," her deep, heavily accented voice intoned as she tapped the stage with a slender white baton, keeping time with the music. Dressed in a black leotard, black stockings, and a pink, knee-length, ballet skirt with a bow tied at her waist, Madame cut a striking figure with her flame-red hair and lips. "First position: Turn de feet out; tuck in de 'ips and de tummy. Plié. Bend de knees. Turn; bend zee arm at de elbow. Lift your hand, gracefully, gracefully. Smile to your audience; you are zee queen. Bend back. Stand straight. Second position..."

Bonnie and Boo were dressed in black leotards, pink tights, and pink kids ballet slippers with tiny, cord bows on top. Bonnie felt pretty and dainty in her ballet outfit. Ballet class was followed by a brief break to allow students to change into their tap shoes.

In addition to ballet, Madame taught tap class. While not as heavily populated as ballet class, the tap dance class had its fair share of members. With discipline and clarity, she led the class in a series of toe taps and heel brushes, each designed to elicit a particular sound. Madame carefully positioned each child's hands and arms for the perfect effect. While monitoring their children, parents sat in the audience chatting quietly with one another. After an hour of dance classes, Beily bundled up the children, put Skipper in the stroller, and headed down to Woolworth's for hot dogs and drinks for lunch. Beily would stand at the end of the counter where Negroes had to wait to be served. She'd place the order, pay for it, and then share the hot dogs among herself and the children. None of them ate a whole hot dog, so two dogs and a coke was more than enough to satiate the four of them.

Next stop: Dry Goods. Wilmington Dry Goods was a gigantic, six-floor, discount, department store. Whatever you needed – clothing, housewares, music, perfume – it was in Dry Goods. This particular day, Beily was hunting down underwear for the children. The children's department always had large display tables chock-full of girls and boys underpants, undershirts, socks, and long johns. Boo needed undershirts to keep her chest warm, and Skipper was outgrowing everything at an alarming rate, so it was time to replenish their wardrobes. Quickly, Beily sorted through a bin, separating Carter's undershirts from the less heavy, off-brand shirts. After selecting the best of the lot for each in her brood, Beily gathered the underwear and children, and trooped off to the cashier.

"Mommy, can we have peanuts?" Bonnie asked. "Daddy always gets peanuts to keep our hands warm."

"If it's on the way, Bonnie." But Beily turned north on Market Street, and Bonnie knew the peanut man was in the opposite direction. Silently, Bonnie followed her mommy, holding on to the side of the stroller while Boo sat on the basket built into the rear of the stroller. Originally designed to carry packages, it was the perfect space for Boo to ride in without complaint.

Two blocks north, Beily turned into Arthur's, a small department store. She loved Arthur's, particularly the hosiery department, which comprised at least 30 percent of the first-floor space. A trip to the hosiery department was like a trip to another planet. The department had a long counter, crowded from end to end with women old and young of every color, shape, and hue you could imagine. Along the wall that rose above the counter was a line of mannequins' bodiless legs with toes pointing to the ceiling like an inverted chorus line. Every leg had a different color hose. Some had seams; some did not. Some were textured; some were sheer. Punctuating the counter were about six metal stands with mini stockings on them. These were just big enough for a woman to slip her hand into them to see how a given shade might look on her legs or against a particular shoe or fabric. This was one of Beily's favorite places to spend time on Saturdays... and one of Bonnie's least favorite. How in the world anyone could spend what seemed like hours trying on color after color after color was beyond Bonnie's understanding. Barely There, Pewter, Grey Mist... the names all began to merge in Bonnie's mind after a while. But Beily really seemed to get energized as she tried each swatch, oohing and aahing as the saleswoman brought out the newest selections in the thin, flat boxes lined with tissue paper and creased over the top of the stockings and beneath. After what seemed like a lifetime, Beily paid for the stockings and left with several boxes, tied neatly with a cord and handle.

"Okay, Bonnie and Boo, one last stop." After heading down Eighth Street and taking a left turn onto King Street, she opened the door to a floor strewn with sawdust. The air was cold, and men wearing white jackets over their clothes with rubber aprons tied around their waists were busy helping customers with their orders. "A pound of flounder and a pound of scallops," Beily said to the man at the counter. "Double-wrap the flounder, please. It has to travel a ways." After paying for the fish and receiving her package, Beily wheeled her brood along King Street north to the parking lot.

As they approached the end of the block, Beily noticed the peanut man standing on the corner with a glass box full of warm peanuts on top of a roaster. She bought two small bags of peanuts, then said, "To keep your hands warm, like daddy does," putting a few peanuts in each of their pockets. Skipper was knocked out in this stroller from a combination of fresh air and too much shopping.

Upon reaching the Ford woodie station wagon, Beily put Boo on the backseat with a blanket, and Skipper slid into his car seat. She put Bonnie in the front seat next to her, then folded the stroller and her packages and put them in the trunk. Exhausted, Beily eased herself behind the wheel and sighed deeply. With any luck, the kids would sleep all the way home. She turned on the radio and listened to Jackie Wilson sing "Lonely Teardrops" as she pulled away.

Chapter 6

FLYING HIGH

As Bonnie was growing older, Beily was beginning to let her play in the backyard more frequently without being out there with her. As Boo and Skip were still babies, they remained in the playpen while Beily finished her cleaning tasks. There was a lot to see and do in the backyard, and Bonnie was happy to have the time and space to explore on her own. There were bugs to dig up and flowers to pick, mud pies to make and cars to watch, and the postman to query. The world was pretty exciting. Just when things couldn't get any better, one day a boy appeared looking through the hedges at Bonnie with a mischievous grin and no front teeth. "Boo!" he said when he knew he had Bonnie's attention. He was taller than Bonnie with curly hair and pretty brown skin, and she asked who he was. "I'm Lee," he replied, "and I have a sister." "Where is she?" Bonnie asked. "Wait; I'll get her. Sister!" he hollered at the top of his lungs. "Sister!" Bonnie could hear him holler off in the distance. Shortly thereafter, the boy reappeared, dragging behind him a pretty little girl with curly braids saying, "Lee, don't run so fast! Stop pulling me. You're making my dress dirty! Stop, Lee. Stop!" "Here she is," the boy announced, presenting his sister like a fisherman showing his prize catch. "This is Sister!" he proudly said. Dusting off her skirt and rubbing the tops of her shoes on the backs of her legs, the little girl extended her hand and said, "I am Mary Louisa Johnson, and this is my brother, Lee. Let's play."

Mary Lou took Bonnie's hand, and off they went. They did all of the things little girls do. Bonnie brought out her dolls and her tea set. They made a table out of napkins and served all their guests, both real and imaginary. Lee cooperated for a while but soon tired of the girls' organized play. Eventually, he ran off and came back with another buddy, Carl Cofrancisco, and the two of them turned around in circles on the lawn until they made themselves sick. They fell on the ground, laughing hysterically, too weak to stand. Then they took off for the wooded lot next door to search for worms and other creepy-crawlies. Of course, they returned after a while and chased Mary Lou and Bonnie around the yard with their insects, threatening to put them in the girls' hair. The girls squealed and shrieked and ran for their lives. Having more fun than their hollering revealed, they collapsed in the center of the yard. Soon they could hear a woman calling, "Lee! Mary Lou! Children! It's time to come home. It's Mommy Lee. We have to go." As she took Lee's hand and started toward the sidewalk, she promised, "We'll come back tomorrow." "Me too," said Carl. *I surely hope so,* Bonnie thought. Because she wasn't allowed to leave the yard, she couldn't walk to their house... yet. The world beyond was mighty big, and frankly, Bonnie was a bit scared to enter into it yet.

Mary Lou, Lee, and Bonnie became fast friends. They spent many hours visiting each other's homes, and Mary Lou became the big sister Bonnie never had, sharing with her all the things that sisters, not moms, did about coming into womanhood, the things that make you blush when your mother explains them. Many Lou also showed her the hip way to do such things as bop, and how to get into a bathtub full of hot water with Wrangler jeans on so that when they dried, they "fit" her backside to a tee. Bonnie had to be careful about how tight she let her Wranglers get, though. Her nana did not appreciate young ladies' letting their "boogie annies," or rear ends, show too much. (I've often wondered what Nana would think about all the "boogie annies," both female and male, we see hanging out of young folks' pants today.)

Mary Lou, Lee, and Bonnie also attended the same high school and church, as well as the Episcopal Young Church group together, where they danced, tried on lipstick, and swooned at the guys.

When she grew up, Mary Louisa became a shapely, attractive young woman. She was known to cause grown men of all racial persuasions to drive over sidewalks with their cars as they watched her walk down the street in her Wranglers, totally oblivious to the effect she was having on the male libido. In high school, she was the second Negro girl to become a cheerleader, which was no mean feat in 1963. Never one to achieve an honor solely for herself, Mary Lou selflessly trained Bonnie, Wanda Ward, and Luz Prado the summer of 1965 in preparation for the cheerleader tryouts at Wilmington High School. Miss McCluskey, the gym teacher, had been in charge of the cheerleaders as far back as the late 1930s and 1940s. As such, she had been responsible for writing many of the cheers and creating the distinctive moves that defined the Wilmington High style of cheering. She had instituted a lot of gymnastics and tumbling in the routines, and she was wary of the rhythm and blues moves that some of the younger folks where anxious to include in the cheers. Earning a spot on the squad could be difficult, and of course, there was always the extra ten pounds to worry about versus the cute factor that some of the blond, petite, and perky candidates could offer. But thanks to Bonnie's ballet and the lessons at the Walnut Street Y many years ago, she could do a cartwheel and a roundoff with the best of them.

So Bonnie, Wanda, and Luz cheered and clapped and grunted for four days a week the whole month of August in the basement of Mary Lou's home. How Mrs. Johnson stood the screams and grunts no one will ever know. She was an elementary schoolteacher preparing lesson plans. It's a wonder she could think, let alone write through that noise. They all became members of the cheering squad, and Luz became the first Puerto Rican to serve as a cheerleader there.

The next spring, Mary Lou graduated from high school, and she matriculated at Morgan State University in Baltimore, Maryland. Upon graduation, she became the first Negro woman – or, by then, Negroes were referred to as blacks – to become a stewardess for Pan American Airways. The neighborhood was so proud of her looking clean and sharp in her uniform, traveling the world, and living a glamorous life. Many Lou Johnson gave new meaning to the words "I'll fly away." She let us know how high and how far we each could go, and she did the job well.

Chapter 7

THE FAIRY TALE MANSION

The red rancher was finally ready. Richard had finished building his fairy tale mansion for his queen, princesses, and prince. In the summer of 1955, Beily and the children moved to 10 Ogden Road, Claymont, Delaware. It was a beautiful home that sat high on a hill, opposite a wooded creek area. Behind the house was a huge lawn with a patio and a play set. Richard had designed and built the home himself. It had the latest appliances – all electric, along with beautiful, oak cabinets and a lovely pink, white, and black Formica kitchen set with a blue and white, linoleum floor in patterned squares. And wonder of wonders, it had a fallout shelter, fully stocked, in the basement. If the commies showed up at the rancher and we survived a nuclear attack, Richard was prepared to protect his family. Unable to secure a mortgage in Delaware with his veterans benefits, Richard had secured one in Chester, Pennsylvania. He performed all his banking there until he passed away some sixty years later, having never forgotten the prejudice he experienced in the icy "Diamond State," which glittered only for whites.

Claymont was different from 301. The house was flat, and you could run through the whole house in a big circle. You even could ride a tricycle around in it, but after the furniture got settled, you could only ride your bikes in the basement. The house was painted sage green and rose inside – Colonial colors, Richard called them. As a gift, Nana had purchased a baby grand piano. She, Beily, and Richard had gone to Pennsylvania to select it and arranged for delivery. Beily had a small, brass plaque engraved that read *"TO BONNIE, BOO AND SKIP, WITH LOVE, NANA."* The plaque was screwed into the center of the music bracket, and the children saw it every time they practiced the piano. Also inside, Richard had built two huge planters and put rubber trees in them. They framed the picture window opposite the fireplace in the living room. A lovely tapestry hung on the wall behind the piano, framing it perfectly. The master bedroom had a new bedroom suite with French provincial furniture made of solid mahogany that Richard had purchased for Beily as a surprise welcome home gift. The master bedroom had wall-to-wall carpeting, but the rest of the house had oak hardwood floors that gleamed like glass.

The Byrds moved into this lovely nest, right next to a lot with a house Richard had purchased for his parents, Sarah and Lee Byrd. Richard had built a three bedroom, white stucco home for them. The two properties were contiguous and resembled a compound separated from the balance of Ogden Road by a huge wooded area.

Sarah and Lee were southern transplants, just like Nana. Lee was a World War I veteran who returned home from Europe to find that Jim Crow still reigned in the South and, in fact, was threatening his home. Lee worked hard at Worth Steel every day, until a steel ingot fell on his left leg, damaging it severely. Then, there was no workers' compensation or disability, so the household was supported by Richard, whom Lee and Sarah still referred to as Airee D. Lee spent most of his days visiting old friends and family on "The Row," the strip of housing Worth Steel built for colored steel workers in the 1920s. He was particularly fond of visiting his brother, Henry; his wife, Daisy; and their rambunctious group of five children. Affectionately known as Grandpop by Bonnie, Boo, and Skip, Lee Byrd was a quiet, steadying force in his home and with his sons. The children loved him, and they could always count on him to find a piece of candy, deep in his pocket, or a piece of fried chicken in the refrigerator to nibble. Grandpop was known for his colloquial, southern speech, and listening to him was like taking your eyes and ears to Hay-vanna in the early 1900s. His references to "young'uns" and "I reckons" introduced the children to a whole new dialect and interpretation of the world. Often, he would sing his old songs, "skay nonnie nonnie, skay nonnie nonnie, skay," to the children's laughter.

His wife, Sarah Byrd, was like a little brown wren. Tiny in stature (four feet ten inches or so) and bony, with chocolate brown skin, a wide nose, thin lips, beady little brown eyes rimmed in pale blue, and straight black bobbed hair in a hairnet, Sarah was the picture of anxiety and discomfort. She did not have a comfortable lap for sitting because she was so thin, and always laughed nervously. Sarah and Beily maintained an uneasy alliance, with the man they both loved, Richard, in the middle. Gramma, as she was known to the children, was the secret-keeper. She said little, but her deep-set eyes, dancing furtively from one place to the next, watched and knew all. Sarah missed home, with its warm days and the Spanish moss cascading from the trees like gray lace. She missed the fresh oranges, warm from the sun, and she missed her family. While her mother, Coote Robinson, was a fearful creature, she had fond memories of her sisters: Lula, better known as Mitja; Ellen aka Dixie; and Rosa referred to as Sister. Sarah, the eldest daughter of the three siblings, had inherited Coote's gift of clairvoyance, or the prophetic. Coote was a beautiful full-blooded Seminole Indian with mahogany brown skin and straight glossy hair. She was a real looker, but she had a scary side, too; she was a shaman, a witch doctor. Her reputation was so fearful that white folks got scared when Coote was around. Her evil eye was known to result in trouble or bad luck, or worse. Richard spoke of how she'd disciplined him and his brother, Roosevelt, when they were children. Disobedience meant Coote would hold your hands in the fire. Literally. Needless to say, as children, they rarely disobeyed her. They may not have lived to tell about it.

Sarah spent some time cleaning and cooking in white folks' homes, most notably the Cauffiels. She spent much of her free time with her niece Daisy Parks. Daisy was a high school graduate and valedictorian, who'd come to visit her Aunt Sarah one summer and fallen in love with Henry Byrd, Lee's youngest brother. While Daisy's family was not happy, Daisy was on her way to college in the fall, so there was nothing to be done. Daisy and Henry married, and they were in Claymont loving each other and raising their children, Henry Jr., Clarence, Barbara, Gwendolyn, and Clifton, the best they could.

Sarah carried her pain and depression sadly and quietly. She drank a little gin, dipped a little snuff, and sipped Pepsi mixed with sugar in a can. It was just enough to keep life a little fuzzy and very internal. She spoke very little, confided in no one, and was completely dependent on Lee and Richard. During the '50s and '60s, colored people were always in pain. Jim Crow, segregation, social ostracism, and limited opportunity in general would've driven anyone into depression, at the very least. So, no one observed Sarah's pain as anything unique, though it was absorbed by her sons, Richard and Roosevelt. An unspoken melancholia surrounded them, their mates, their children, and their work lives. It was like a fog, sometimes faint, sometimes thick, but palpable and ever existent. Sometimes the fog threatened to kill them all, erupting into drunken violence, denials, and lies. But in the clearings and when the fog lifted, it was an idyllic life and one they enjoyed.

Chapter 8

RUNNING AWAY FROM HOME

In Claymont, life moved at a whole different pace than in the city at 301. There were no streetlights to speak of. The roads were narrow, turtle-backed, and traffic rarely passed through. Bonnie knew what time it was by the sounds of the steel mill located about a mile away. The red rancher's backyard was connected to Bonnie's grandparents' house, with the only separation being the large driveway between the two houses that connected to the garage at the rear of the new home, so Bonnie, Boo, and Skip could run freely between the two properties at will. Gramma grew grapes and a small vegetable garden. If she picked them before the heat of the day, Bonnie could pull sassafras tea roots right out of the ground and pull the stamen from the honeysuckle to get the one drop of sweetness before the bees. The property also had huge wild blackberry bushes, and Gramma often baked her "blackberry dooby," with large, fluffy dumplings, just for the children. She always strained the berries carefully in cheesecloth so there were never any of those tiny seeds left behind, sticking in between the teeth, and the syrup was a clear, deep purple. Now, that was love – those extra little steps in food preparation performed just because she loved Bonnie, Boo, and Skip that much, love as basic and warm as home cooking could ever get.

The Byrd grandparents were a study in the effects leaving the South had on the first generation of The Great Migration participants. They were hard-working, thrifty, pushing work, and saw education for their children and land ownership as the ultimate freedom. No one ever mentioned or looked for the forty acres and a mule or reparations, as you hear of today. Lee and Sarah Byrd were more of the "just tell me where Mr. Cholly is going to be so I can get the Sam

Hill out of the way and live." They were sweet, peaceful people who just wanted to live out their lives, in quiet, surrounded by family.

Uncle Roosevelt, nicknamed "Rokie" or "Roke," also lived with Lee and Sarah, as did his daughter, Sandy. Uncle Rokie had been a handsome, rather dashing young man in his teens and youth. He was funny and gifted and sought after by many a young woman. However, all of that changed with the war. Sent to North Africa as part of the troops General George S. Patton was responsible for, Uncle Rokie came home a broken man. He was quiet, nearly silent, and his eyes spoke volumes. They had seen pain, sorrow, and destruction that was unfathomable. He had retreated deep into the recesses of his soul, never to exit again. He rarely spoke and basically limited his responses to a monosyllabic code consisting of yes, no, and grunts. It was so painful to watch him and his brother, Richard, interact because Richard could remember when their relationship was different... when they would drive their car and pick up the girls so eagerly awaiting their attentions.

Now Uncle Rokie's attentions focused narrowly on an amber-colored pint bottle of Red Rose whiskey. He existed in a world pleasantly softened by the haze the liquor created. It made the blows of life easier to endure, but it gnawed away at the person Richard and his parents loved so much. To the contrary, Richard never drank liquor. In fact, he hated it and advised all his children to never touch it. "You have too much Indian in you," he'd say. "It'll kill you." Later, Boo and Skip found out they lacked the gene necessary to digest alcohol, so there was truth to this statement.

The war had to have been difficult for Lee and Sarah, as both of their young sons were sent to war. They were protective of their sons, and the war took their children far away, beyond their protective arms and home. Lee had served in World War I, so he had some idea of what his sons would encounter. All that Sarah could anticipate was a long absence, fear, and another reason to worry.

In Claymont, summer days were hot and humid. At that time, no one had an air conditioner in his or her home. You were considered wealthy if you had a fan or two in the window or, even better, a big, round one in the middle of the floor that graciously blew air on any lucky soul in its path. On days like this, people moved slowly. Sarah carried a fan, and she and Lee drank lots of lemon water and sat on the porch. Heavy work, such as laundry and ironing, was done early in the morning in the basement, where it was cool before the heat and humidity grew to be too much. On these days, the children played inside or on the patio until the sun got high. Then they played in the large open basement, riding their bikes and tricycles round and round until dinnertime.

The most important daily visitor was the postman. Bonnie met him at the mailbox at the foot of the hill every day, waiting to see what he would bring. Beily had gotten her a subscription to the *Weekly Reader*, and she felt grown up having her own paper delivered to her at home. Bonnie would read it cover to cover, over and over again, until it literally fell apart. While Beily was busy sewing her dresses for school in the fall, and Bonnie was learning to make dresses for her dolls, her most important time was spent reading anything she could get her hands on. In fact, Beily took the three children to the library once a week in Wilmington. They could go down to the undercroft of the big library on Rodney Square, where all the children's books were housed. The bonus was that it was extremely cool there because it was built in the basement of the building. Bonnie had her own library card, which Beily kept in her wallet. For one hour, Bonnie meandered all around the library, pulling out books that interested her. She read a lot of classics, such as *Black Beauty*, *Nancy Drew* and *The Hardy Boys*. Most of all, she was really into adventure and travel to foreign lands and other time periods. It was all about escape. She had no one to play with except her sister, Boo, and her brother, Skip. Because they were two or more years younger, they seemed like babies, and most of the time, Bonnie was responsible for helping Beily look after them.

However, when she crawled into a good book, Bonnie was somewhere else. She was not in Claymont, and she was not hot. She was solving a murder or eating porridge in Victorian England. Bonnie was in her own world.

Unbeknownst to her parents, Bonnie was reading pretty well, and she had learned how to look up the meanings of words in a dictionary her dad had brought her. One evening, he brought home a paper with a picture of a white man with thinning hair. The headline read "ELMO SMITH RAPES AND KILLS CHILD." These were new concepts to Bonnie. Rape, murder, and child didn't fit together in her worldview. So Bonnie asked her mom what it meant. She looked puzzled and asked, "Where did Bonnie learn this?" "Why, the paper, Mom," she replied. "It's right there across the top." Her dad looked up from the repair he was working on in the kitchen, clearly alarmed. "He was a bad man, Bonnie. He can't hurt anybody now. Go play with Boo and Skip." Once he thought she was out of earshot, he commented to Beily, "We'd better keep the paper away from her for a while."

But in her mind, Bonnie knew something really had to have been wrong. They'd never tried to stop her from reading anything. Usually they were overjoyed if she read the cake box. *Knowledge is a two-edged sword*, Bonnie reflected. This situation must really be bad. So, of course, she made it her objective to read the paper every day to follow Elmo's trial. She read all the gory details, scaring herself to the point that she couldn't sleep at night. Every sound of the night -- the crickets, the frogs, and the occasional car -- made her cringe in fear.

Meanwhile, Richard and Beily's relationship was starting to crumble. Richard was angry more and more often. Beily wanted to get her nurse practitioner's license and had been attending evening classes at the University of Pennsylvania, but Richard clearly was not supportive of the idea. He was also unhappy about her participation in the Playcrafters at the church, St. Matthew's Episcopal, in Wilmington. It was pretty tight, emotionally, and sometimes the pot boiled over in angry words and behaviors.

Sometimes Richard just left and didn't return for days. Beily had no one to really talk to because all the other women in Claymont whom she was close to were in similar, if not worse, predicaments. Nana believed Beily had made a choice, and now she had to stick with it, so Nana had no sympathy for her.

The marriage labored on. Like a chicken with its head cut off, the marriage ran on for a while, not realizing it was dead. But, you could see it in Beily's eyes. Bonnie could tell by the indifference between them even more than by the occasional white-hot anger and crackle of fear that tore through the house. The lack of touch between her parents, the absence of laughter, the slow, but steady, loss of weight until Momma was just skin and bones. Beily was a woman who should have been loved and hugged and kissed often, and Richard just was not capable of that kind of love. What attracted her to him was dying and unlikely to be revived, choked off by unexplained anger and fear and psychoses resulting from the war and left untreated. Somehow, Bonnie could feel all this tension. Her reaction was she developed eczema all over her hands and arms. Her sister developed asthma. Her brother was oblivious.

One morning, in the midst of Elmo Smith and her parents' disintegrating marriage, Bonnie awoke early, made a peanut butter sandwich, wrapped it carefully in waxed paper, and put it inside a scarf she knotted as a kerchief. Later that day, she found a stick and tied the kerchief to it like a hobo had done in one of the books she'd read. She stored the whole contraption under her bed. She'd wait and leave later. Bonnie needed to escape it all. That night, she went to sleep with the travelers bag under the covers with her. Her mommy must have seen the stick when she tucked her in because when she woke up the next morning, Bonnie found Beily sitting by her bedside with tears in her eyes. "Bonnie Aileen, where were you going, and why?" How does a kid tell her mother, "Mom, I'm really having anxiety attacks about the stress between you and daddy"? And "I feel like the bottom is going to drop out. I'm afraid of the anger between you, and I feel like I'm gonna pop wide open! Help! Get us outta here, and NOW!" Nope, she couldn't say that, so instead, Bonnie said, "Oh, Mommy, I was so afraid of Elmo Smith. I just had to get away." "Bonnie, why didn't you tell me this? He is locked up. He cannot hurt you or any other little girl ever again. Please do not ever try to do something like this again. I would be very, very sad." She put her arms around Bonnie and held her close. Bonnie started to cry and wail. "Oh, Mommy, I was too scared to leave. It was dark." Beily rocked Bonnie until she calmed down. By this time, Boo and Skipper were awake and at the side of her bed.

"You can be sure I wouldn't go with her!" said Skip. "Bonnie, you are crazy! There are lions and tigers out there. You must be nuts." Temporarily insane? Not really. Just a little girl trying to reach peace. But Bonnie never tried to run away again. She never wanted to make her momma cry again. Not ever.

Chapter 9

GOIN' TO TAMPA, Y'ALL

Richard Byrd was from the Plantation, Havana, located near Apopka, Florida, close to the western panhandle of the state. His mother's sister, Rosa, maintained a home there as did his father's uncle, Arthur. It was important to Richard that his family meet his wife, Beily, and their three children. So, it was determined that the northern branch of the Byrds would make the drive from Claymont to Tampa sometime during the summer. Most trips were a pleasant point of interest, happily anticipated and planned for eagerly. However, that was decidedly not the case for this trip. There seemed to be extra special planning, car maintenance, food packing, and so on, but most of all there was the palatable taste and smell of fear. Something about the sharpness in Richard's voice, the pitch in Beily's responses, and the soberness in the way the preparations were carried out in a quiet, almost secret-like way let Bonnie know that this trip was not such a pleasant one for their family.

They left in the dark of night, passing through Washington, D.C., careful to stop and refill the gas tank before reaching the Virginia border. Boo and Skip were in the way back of the navy blue woodie station wagon Beily drove. Sandwiched in between the suitcases and basket of goodies, they looked like two little brown angels with damp, tight curls around the edges of their faces. Bonnie was in the middle seat. Ever watchful, she wanted to make sure her mommy and dad were okay. As they pulled out of the gas station, Bonnie heard her dad say, "Now Beily, I know you don't like it, but I need you to put that makeup on now." Beily looked so unhappy as she pulled out a compact with very dark powder in it. She carefully applied it to her face. "Mommy, why are you putting that mud on?" Bonnie asked. The makeup was much darker than her mother's complexion, and she looked really strange to Bonnie. "That's to protect us," said Dad. Puzzled, Bonnie didn't know what to say, so she got quiet. "Now sit back and away from the light, Beily," Richard said. Bonnie was really confused now. She knew her dad was proud of his beautiful wife. This behavior was unprecedented. Years later, Bonnie realized Richard was afraid of her mom being mistaken as white. A Negro man caught traveling with a white woman in the South in the early 1950s could end up lynched at the end of a rope on a tree. Emmett Till's picture in *Jet* magazine left a searing memory for any colored person who could see. Bonnie did the only thing she knew to do. She wrapped her arms around their necks and hugged them as they rode into the darkness. They drove through the night. No one spoke, and the radio didn't function except for something sounding like white noise and crackling. The Byrd family made one stop in North Carolina to fill up the gas tank and to use the colored bathrooms. Then it was on to Tampa. They pulled into Uncle Arthur's orange grove as the sun began to rise. Both of Bonnie's parents let out an audible, "Whew."

Uncle Arthur's house was a new, sparkly white, stucco rancher. Beily, Boo, and Bonnie stayed at Aunt Rosa's house, which was older, much shabbier, and very damp. Her hospitality was warm and inviting, though, so they were happy to receive her kindness after the tense trip south. Aunt Rosa had something that Uncle Arthur didn't – their cousin Marshelle lived with Aunt Rosa. Marshelle was beautiful, friendly, and funny. She was the color of milk chocolate with long, dark, wavy hair. When she spoke, it sounded like melted butter with syrup dripping. She spoke her words slowly and languidly. Also, she frequently said "Y'all" and by the time the family left Tampa a week later, Boo and Bonnie were saying it too. They used this expression for many years after that visit, despite their dad's frequent correction.

Marshelle, Boo, and Bonnie played outside all day long. The trees were full of Spanish moss, which swept the ground like a long, formal gown, and made for great places to play hide-and-seek. The girls ate oranges, warm from the sun, out of the grove until the juice ran from the corners of their mouths in sticky rivulets. Beily declared that oranges were coming out of their ears. They swatted mosquitoes as big as small babies, and they ate barbecue ribs until the sauce ran over their bibbed shorts like red stripes. Life was good in Tampa, and the people were sweet, just like Grandpop had said.

Soon, too soon, it was time to go home. It was their first and last visit to see Richard's family in Florida, and Bonnie's first and last exposure to deep southern segregation. She had to go home to Claymont to experience segregation northern-style as a second-grader at Green Street Elementary School. And it wasn't so sweet.

Chapter 10

THE MOST VALUABLE LESSON

During the winter months, life in Claymont became a lot more difficult. Bonnie attended the First Line School, a segregated single-room school for colored children grades one through eight there. Boo and Skip were cared for at St. Michael's Day Nursery during the day in Wilmington. Richard and Beily drove into town to work at their assigned public schools. Usually, Bonnie waited in her Aunt Daisy's kitchen for her mom or dad to pick her up at the end of the day, or she walked about a quarter of a mile to her grandparents' home if they were going to be available. However, one particular day, Bonnie's mother had her take the bus from Claymont to downtown Wilmington to meet her at St. Michael's Day Nursery. Bonnie had no idea why she had to do this, but it was necessary to facilitate something her mom had to do. So at the ripe old age of six, Bonnie walked about a mile from school to her house at the end of Hickman Row; then she walked another mile along Ogden Road, where the two Byrd properties were located at the junction of Naamans Road and the Philadelphia Pike.

At this time, the path she followed was largely rural. The roadway from the school to Hickman Row was lined with persimmon and crab apple trees. Also, you could see the neat, individual vegetable gardens the residents of Hickman Row cultivated on the raised earthen tiers even with the rooftops of their homes. You could hear the pigs grunt and the hens cluck, too. The Row itself was quiet, lined thick with trees on one side of the highway with a lone brick hall-cum-church on the opposite side of the street from the town houses. Past The Row, thick trees formed an archway over the highway until you reached the two Byrd properties, and then the road sloped steeply past Dr.

Wilson's mansion, with the hanging tree where escaping slaves who failed to reach the Pennsylvania border were hung. Then the road curved sharply to the left as it exited onto Naamans Road, which had only two commercial establishments – a candy store on the right and a liquor store on the left – from that point to the Philadelphia Pike, the major thoroughfare into Wilmington. After crossing the railroad tracks, you reached the big white colonial building known as the Naamans Tea House. Local lore said this is where George Washington had spent the night in Delaware. To the left of the Tea House was a hard, cold slab of rock that you could sit on or step down to the sidewalk that paralleled the dusty turtle backed road.

Realizing she might not be seen in time if she sat on the rock, Bonnie stood up, peering up toward Chester, praying the bus driver would see her and stop. It was lonely out there and a bit cold. Bonnie was frightened. She felt in her pocket for the token her mommy had given her to pay the bus driver. "Bonnie, be sure and let the driver know you must get off at French Street," her mommy said. "Okay," Bonnie said. "I know. I'll do it, Mommy."

Finally, she could see the bus a ways off coming toward her. As it got closer, she waved her arms, glad she had worn her bright red mittens and cap Nana had knitted for her. *Surely, he can see my mittens and cap*, she thought. If he can see a red light, he's got to notice these.

Evidently, the bus driver spied her. He brought the bus to a stop with a wheeze and the sound of gravel grating the highway. After a pop of the crank on the door, Bonnie climbed up the steps, put the token in the pay box, and sat as close to the driver as she could. "Please, Mr. Bus Driver," Bonnie said, "I must get off at French Street to meet my mommy." "Okay, little lady," he said.

Bonnie was so exhausted from the walk and her adventure that she fell asleep as the bus listed from side to side down the highway and rode up and down the hills of the Philadelphia Pike. She awoke with a start to find herself at the foot of French Street facing the train station. She jumped up, crawled onto the seat on her knees, leaned toward the window, and pulled the cord, letting the bus driver know she had to get off at the next stop.

When Bonnie stepped down from the bus, she looked at the train station, turned around, and prayed while she batted back her tears. "Dear God, please don't let me be lost. Please let me walk up this street and find St. Michael's and my mommy." She prayed and walked and prayed and walked. It seemed like she'd walked a long time, but finally she saw St. Michael's Day Nursery ahead. The brick fronts of buildings looked familiar. And yes, there was her mommy and the navy station wagon. Bonnie had made it. She was safe.

Years later, when she was a mother, Bonnie would ask herself how Momma could have expected her to ride the bus alone all the way into town and find her. She was only six years old, and she was so afraid. After Bonnie learned how her momma *was forced* to find a place to stay and work because she thought her mother was dying, Bonnie had a much better understanding. A trip on the bus was nothing compared with the challenge Beily had faced. Even more importantly, after that experience, Bonnie knew she could rely on herself; her own instincts for survival could be trusted to kick in. Some lessons in life are only learned by a lonely struggle. Once you develop the muscle to survive, life continues to offer lessons that require you to up the ante, but the basic instinct remains intact always.

Bonnie is so thankful to Beily for the struggle. It was the most valuable lesson she'd ever taught her.

Chapter 11

FAMILY TIES

Without many friends to speak of, Richard certainly had no one he cared to invite to spend the weekend. So it was amazing to Bonnie that he had invited his friend James "Jimmy" Frances; his wife, Mel, also referred to as Mary Ellen; and their two children, Raymond and Lloyd, to visit their home in Claymont for the weekend. The one clarifying factor was that Jimmy Frances had been a friend of Richard's during "The War." World War II may have ended in the surrender of the Germans and Japanese in 1945, but in Richard Byrd's home, the war never ended. Bonnie, Boo, and Skip knew more about the landing of the Negro troops in Maghull, England, than they did about Negro employment in Delaware before they were five years old. The children learned about the troops crossing in Normandy, laying bombs in France, the battle at Bois de Boulogne, and the Italian resistance, too. "The War" loomed large in Richard's experiences, and it was not too pleasant. It had left him depressed, angry, and cynical. He didn't trust most people and worked hard to provide protection for his parents, wife, and children far from the madding crowd. So the two Byrd households were high on a hill in semi-rural Claymont, separated from the things and people by which Richard felt threatened, which included almost everyone and everything, especially Mr. Cholly and Cuffy.

The Franceses were from Long Island, New York. Mel was from England, and Bonnie gathered that she and Jimmy had met while he was stationed in Maghull as a member of the U.S. Army during "The War." Evidently, Mel was pregnant with their eldest son, Raymond, while they were in Maghull. James had returned to Maghull after the war, married Mel, and brought her to the States.

Tall and thin, Mel had red hair, blue eyes, and thin, unsmiling lips. Her eyes constantly darted around their home lovelessly, taking into account the baby grand piano her nana had purchased for them to learn to play, the carpets, the fine furnishings, and paintings Bonnie's mother had tastefully arranged. She was clearly angry and bitter, and she whispered mean, ugly things to Beily that Bonnie didn't understand, but she grasped that they caused her momma a great deal of pain. Instinctively, Bonnie clung to her mother, using every bit of her seven-year-old frame to wedge between her mommy and Mel. If it's possible to conjure up feelings of hatred at seven years old, that is pretty much what Bonnie felt toward Mel. Bonnie hated that Mel made her mother uncomfortable in her own home, her place of authority and comfort. She hated Mel's tight, smug mouth, and Bonnie hated the way Mel doted on Raymond, her twelve-year-old son, constantly running her fingers through his hair. On the other hand, Mel clearly found her younger son Lloyd's more "Negroid" appearance unacceptable. Lloyd was the same age as Bonnie and full of spunk. He was fair with freckles and brown eyes. His hair was what Negroes called a rhiny reddish blond and kinky like his daddy's hair. He had a mischievous grin and no front teeth. He was the one his dad clearly preferred. Lloyd and Bonnie became buddies and played together a lot that weekend.

In an attempt to show the Franceses a pleasant time, Beily took Mel and her sons to Washington, D.C., that Saturday. Bonnie didn't know where Mr. Frances and Richard went. Somehow their whereabouts were not a significant part of her interests. She did remember it was a cold, overcast day and that the cherry blossoms were in full bloom. She remembered her mom taking pictures with her SLR camera at the Lincoln Memorial and the Washington Monument. Also, Bonnie remembered a brief "pit stop," as her mom called it, at her Aunt Ethel's home in northeast Washington after they had seen all that they could see. It was getting late, and it was a long drive home for two women with five kids in the back of the woodie. After all, these were the 1950s. Women weren't liberated. They came home and had dinner ready for their husbands.

Bonnie remembered Aunt Ethel looking sideways at Mel and muttering, "Where did this white trash come from?" They enjoyed some sips of hot chocolate and applesauce cookies Auntie had made before piling into the car. "Beily, call me when you get home," Aunt Ethel said. "I love you all so much. Give Richard my best!" And then they saw her tiny, petite body in the rear window waving good-bye, and Uncle Mooney, her huge, six-foot-four second husband, standing next to her, peering after them as they drove away.

Mel and Jimmy and the kids left early the next morning for New York. They never visited again, and if Richard visited Mr. Frances thereafter, he never shared it with Beily or the kids. Bonnie had the distinct feeling that whatever had transpired during that visit had created deep fissures in her parents' marital bond. The mere mention of either of the Franceses brought a look to Beily's face of hurt and anger, and she drew her lips into a thin, tight line as though to physically stay any word on the topic from escaping her lips. Beily never did that when anything else was discussed.

Bonnie wouldn't understand the snide remarks from Mel until some fifty-plus years had passed, when her dad revealed that she had a brother that had been born in England through a relationship he'd had with a young British woman when he was an eighteen-year-old soldier who had just landed in Maghull. This was the first time he had been treated like a man, not a colored. Richard was one handsome bugger. He often recounted how the girls would run out to greet them. Their color didn't matter. It had been a long time since these young women had seen men, let alone young men, in their villages. According to Richard, huge dances to the latest music and bands were held nightly in Maghull, and as music, moonlight, romance, and hormones would have it, folks became attracted to one another, and lots of babies were created.

Bonnie, Boo, and Skip's brother, James Dunne, was the result of such a relationship. He was born in Maghull to Irene Dunne on September 5, 1943. He was raised to believe that his grandparents were his parents and that his mother was his sister. It wasn't until his grandparents died that he discovered a strong box containing his original birth certificate, listing his father as Richard Byrd, Negro, U.S. Army. At that point, he realized all he had been told about his heritage was untrue. Jim began searching online for the whereabouts of Richard Byrd. He was devastated to learn his father had passed just before he learned of his whereabouts.

On the American side of the Atlantic, as Richard knew he was approaching the end of his life, he told Bonnie and her brother, Richard Lee, that they had a brother in England. He made them promise that they would find him and tell him that he loved him. Bonnie was a bit shocked, yet intrigued, by the revelation. This certainly explained the years of her father's annual, unexplained months-long trips on the QE2 to England to visit old war buddies. It explained why he never told Bonnie, Boo, or Richard Lee who the buddies were or even where he stayed while in England. As he grew older and more fragile, as his forgetfulness increased, it became frightening to think of him wandering around England unescorted and uncared-for.

One day, Richard Lee received a call at his office asking if Richard Byrd was there and if he had been in World War II. His receptionist replied no. The questioning continued and became more personal, so the receptionist asked Richard Lee to take the call personally. After some discussion, the caller revealed that she was from the American Red Cross and that she was calling on behalf of James Dunne, who was seeking his father. Before contact could be established, certain papers had to be signed. After agreeing to sign the paperwork and mail it by airmail, Richard Lee, somewhat stunned, called Bonnie to share what had transpired.

They made arrangements to meet in New York when Jim would be traveling on business. Bonnie's husband, Alton, and her brother, Richard Lee, gathered, waiting for the appointed meeting at 8 PM in the hotel lobby. Bonnie was as nervous as a cat. What would Jim be like? Would he accept us? Would we be able to tell we were related?

Bonnie walked down a hall of the hotel toward the lobby. A tall, lean, handsome man approached her. Something within her leaped. "Jim, is that you?" she asked. "Why, hullo, Bonnie. It is Bonnie, isn't it?" And spontaneously they embraced. In one hug, they crossed oceans, they healed racial prejudice and injustice, and Richard's eldest son came home. Bonnie knew her dad could finally be at peace in his eternal rest.

They walked back down the hall to the hotel lounge, where her husband and brother waited. When Jim and Bonnie entered the room, her brother smiled a big, broad grin. "Hey, big brother," Richard Lee said as they embraced. Al just stood observing and nodding his head in agreement. He and Jim embraced and exchanged hellos.

Richard Lee and Bonnie sat back and watched a paler version of their dad in action. He walked like their dad; he moved like their dad; he even wore a gold chain bracelet on his left arm like their dad. Dear Lord, those Byrd genes were strong! Jim was tall, six foot four, slender, and handsome with olive skin and wavy hair. He was well-spoken with a soft, pleasant British accent that had a slight Irish lilt. At one point in the evening, when they took pictures, Alton had Jim and Richard Lee sit side by side. It was eerie, like a positive and negative photo of their dad. The evening passed pleasantly. Slowly and carefully, a bridge was built, heart to heart, among us. Lifelong bonds and bloodlines were established, paving the way for many more reunions and a lifetime of happy family memories.

Chapter 12

THE MOVE TO TERMINAL AVENUE

Over the past several months, the pressure between Richard and Beily had risen to a fever pitch. The lies, unexplained absences, anger, and control issues had expanded the cracks between them into a space as broad as the Grand Canyon. No longer able to withstand the madness or bridge the distance, Beily decided to move out of the rancher at 10 Ogden Road. She had begged Nana to let her return to 301, but Nana's position was because Beily was married, she should work it out. "You have made your bed; now lie in it" was the way of handling matters such as this. So Beily stuck it out the best she could, until she could no longer handle it. Then, she and the children moved into a rickety third-floor apartment in an old home on Terminal Avenue in New Castle, Delaware. The apartment was not comparable to her usual standard of living, but Beily was seeking safety and peace of mind more than anything else. The tension at 10 Ogden Road was unbearable. Bonnie had eczema everywhere. Little Boo experienced increased asthma attacks. Only Skipper was oblivious to things, and she was grateful for that.

The Whittingtons were their new next-door neighbors. Gratefully, they had two lovely children: Ronnie, who became Bonnie's best buddy, and Joyce, who played with Boo and Skip, depending on availability and whether Skip was up for playing with girls that day.

The neighborhood was safe and quiet, and had two distinct parts. The upper portion of Terminal Avenue was populated by office workers, schoolteachers, state employees, postal workers, and automobile workers. The stucco, stone, or clapboard single-family dwellings had nicely apportioned yards. Several solidly positioned

Negro middle-class families had begun springing up in the area as white families began selling their properties and purchasing newer homes deeper into New Castle, distancing themselves from the increasing, encroaching Negro population growth. The pressure on this area to expand was created by the Poplar Street Project A. This latest Negro removal program was designed to upgrade the quantity and quality of the housing stock within the East Side of Wilmington. These were the areas of the city where the white Eastern European ethnic communities – the Polish, Lithuanians, and Germans -- had lived close to the factories along Fourth Street and Maryland Avenue. These families began to press into southwest Wilmington – Browntown/Hedgeville – and northwest into the Highlands between Pennsylvania and Delaware Avenues.

The other demographic forces at play were occurring outside of the city's limits. Those forces were the razing of Millside in 1955 and the installation of the first suburban housing development in New Castle County, Delaware, built to address the specific needs of a burgeoning Negro middle class. The development, named Dunleith, was complete with its own brand-new elementary school. But Millside was considered blight on the horizon of this "up-and-coming" group of folks in Dunleith. Therefore, to increase the economic value and attractiveness of Dunleith, Millside and its poorly housed Negro migrants from the South had to have a solution. Simultaneously, the desegregation of public housing in Wilmington presented the first real opportunities for lower economic classes of Negroes to live in decent, safe affordable housing. Together these physical and economic forces combined to bring about the razing of Millside, a former army barracks that had become a slum tenement for poor Negroes migrating north seeking better opportunities and refuge from the harshness of life in the South. Many of its residents had relocated in Wilmington as a second choice for an urban refuge. These families had traveled from other larger, northern cities – Detroit and Chicago – where they had originally relocated, seeking work in the automobile factories there. When their original attempt at relocation from the South was determined unsuccessful, these families began to travel toward the East Coast centers of commerce, such as Delaware, Maryland, New Jersey, and New York.

The other end of Terminal Avenue was the entry to the Wilmington Port Authority. There were about three older homes along the street and a couple of businesses that catered to the port or chemical businesses. Large trucks often barreled down the avenue in this direction to off-load the huge ships arriving at the port from all over the world. Near the end of this section, about a half mile before the Port of Wilmington, was a large older home with a huge surrounding lot that housed the Williams family.

The Williams family included Grandfather Jesse and Grandmother Viola; their daughters, Lola and Nina; and their daughter's children. Various and sundry cousins and friends were always dropping by the house, so there was always something going on. From a child's perspective, this house was an odd mix of the best and the worst life could offer. Here was always someone to play with, and if you got tired of him or her, another cousin was always visiting or a playmate was down the street. The house backed up to a vast wooded field that made an excellent place for staging attacks and wars, building and burning tacky-outs, and occasionally exploring the offices of the small chemical businesses, when all else failed. The rear of the yard contained the kitchen garden – critical to most Southern families – as well as pigpens, a chicken coop, and a smokehouse. Whatever amenities were missing, the Williams family was eating, and eating well.

On the downside, adults were everywhere, laughing, sleeping, gossiping, loving, and always watching you. A kid never got a break. You could be sure if you did something wrong, someone under twelve was going to pay, whether you did it or not. "Spare the rod, and spoil the child" was not happening in this house. The switch and the belt were the disciplinary tools of choice. Worse yet, the victim often was directed, "Boy, go out and get me a good switch so I can whip your behind." Grandmom Williams was good for that one, as she would bite her lower lip and hold you by the top of your head. She would hit you with the switch and swear, "This hurts me more than it hurts you. So hold still while I tear that be-hind up." If you cried, it just made her madder. But she was loving and forgiving, and soon she would be slipping you a piece of cake and a cold glass of milk to take the sting out of things.

In this rough-and-tumble situation, Butch Williams was growing up. He was the good boy, the one to whom everyone else had to measure up. Butch watched his Uncle James, the only son of Viola and Jesse Williams. James had a different life plan and lifestyle. He did not live on Terminal Avenue long. He was studying pharmacy at Howard University in Washington, D.C. He told Butch he wanted a better way of life, and education was the key. Everybody loved and admired James, his books, the good looks. Butch remembered that and took note to perform at the highest level he could in his studies. He liked being distinguished in a positive way. It brought him favor among the adults at home and at school.

Butch also was developing as an athlete, excelling at baseball, basketball, and track. The basis of his character was being developed; he had a polite, pleasant personality, was an academic competitor, and proved to be a superior athlete. These qualities and being born downright cute... well, it can make for the basis of greatness and success.

Early one bright Saturday morning, Butch and several of his male cousins were zooming up and down Terminal Avenue. It was dusty, dirty work, but gee, what fun. He looked up to see Ronnie Whittington, his schoolmate, riding toward him. He waved good-bye to his cousins and pedaled out to meet him.

Ronnie was a husky kid with a wide, easy grin and a soft, "Hey, man" as he braked to a graceful stop on his new bicycle. As they saddled up to one another, each facing opposite directions, Ronnie said, "Listen, I'm having a birthday party later today. I'd like you to come. My mom's making a cake, peach cobbler, and everything." Butch thought for a moment and said enthusiastically, "Yeah, man, I'll be there. What time?" "'Bout two o'clock," Ronnie responded brightly. "Okay. See you then," Butch replied as he pedaled down the road back home.

Butch quickly rode home and gained permission from his mother to attend the party. He bathed and dressed in his Sunday best. Butch was ready for the party. He bounded out the door and was off to Ronnie's. He felt a sense of anticipation as he approached the Whittingtons' front door. He rang the doorbell, smoothing his freshly ironed shirt. Mrs. Whittington came to the door dressed in a crisp apron, capri pants, and a blouse. The kitchen smelled of cakes, pies, and peaches. A beautiful woman who enjoyed her husband, children, and home, she welcomed Butch into the house, and Ronnie and several other kids followed.

Ronnie quickly introduced Butch to the other kids. He knew everybody except one person, a new girl. Her name was Bonnie, Bonnie Byrd... and for some reason, she'd caught his eye. But Ronnie introduced her as his girlfriend as if to let him know she was off-limits. *Hmm*, thought Butch.

The party moved along nicely. Pin the tail on the donkey, cake, and ice cream. Finally, Ronnie's mom cleared the dishes. "You kids play checkers and horseshoes, and then it will be time to go home," she said. Checking to see that Mrs. Whittington was safely ensconced in front of the television, several of the boys, led by Butch, quickly organized the age-old spin the bottle game. As everyone formed a circle, Ronnie sat down and motioned for Bonnie to sit behind him. She looked relieved as she quietly complied. She and Ronnie had become fast friends, playing together every available moment. Ronnie was kind, gentle, and protective, in contrast to his husky build and big-boy ways. He was exactly the type of friend she needed as she tried to reestablish her equilibrium.

But those rowdy hooligans down the street, those were the scary kids, and the boys were wild and bad – although Butch, the one so eagerly organizing the game, seemed to look pretty normal today. He even seemed to have some manners, but thank goodness she didn't have to play, and she knew Ronnie would enforce it. Wouldn't you know, that Butch boy was going to be the first to spin the bottle. *What a name*, Bonnie thought, *a bully's name*, as she did her best to shrink and disappear behind Ronnie's broad back.

"How come she's not playing?" She heard Butch ask Ronnie. "She's my girl," Ronnie said firmly. "Besides, it's my party, and I set the rules." "Hey, man. It's okay. There's plenty of girls here," Butch chuckled. "But you can't blame a guy for asking." He leaned around Ronnie to look Bonnie square in the eye and winked broadly at her. Bonnie giggled in spite of herself, but she didn't budge from her space behind Ronnie.

"Okay, children," Mrs. Whittington called out from the den. "Put the checkers away; time for the party to end and you to go home."

"Umph, umph, umph," grunted Butch. "Oh, well, better luck next time," he said, looking at Bonnie. "See you, man." Bonnie never knew how much a grunt could foretell.

By the end of that summer, Richard's promises to change, and his entreaties and Nana's to return to Claymont and resume the marriage had begun to affect Beily. The limitations of the apartment, a new job as a school nurse for the Wilmington Public School System, and the desire for family all pushed her back to the red rancher. Beily packed up and returned to Claymont to try to be a family once more.

Chapter 13

THE ANNUAL CHURCH PICNIC

Claymont revealed Delaware's southern roots and its "Border State" proclivities. Its outright racist underpinnings were prominently displayed in its school system, which was segregated. In 1956, when the young Byrd family was ready to send Bonnie, its firstborn, to school, colored children had only one option: the State Line School. The school was still run by Pauline Dyson, who had taught the entire generation of those who had migrated north since the early 1900s and landed in Claymont. She was now continuing her service to the community by teaching the offspring of that generation, as well as their grandchildren and great-grandchildren.

State Line School sat in a protected location to the rear of Hickman Row, down an unpaved path about half a mile behind the neat vegetable gardens, chicken coops, and hogpens maintained by the residents of Hickman Row. Every school day, children in first through eighth grade walked the pathway – lined with persimmon trees, crab apple trees, blackberry bushes, and sassafras roots – toward the school. Eventually, the greenery would part, and the path widened. To the left were a couple of older, rusty seesaws, decades old swing sets, and a grove of crab apples. Gradually, the opening cleared into a broad semicircle, with enough space for a car to turn around. A one-story brick building with broad granite steps and white Grecian columns stood to the right of the clearing about a block behind the playground equipment. A large carved wooden door was at the top of the steps, with sidelight windows on either side. It was a fairly grand building for the little semirural colored community for which it was built through the largesse of Pierre S. duPont, a local philanthropist who provided equal education facilities for colored children throughout Delaware.

Having reached the semicircle at the entry to the school, the elementary and junior high schoolchildren of Hickman Row began to gather as the sun climbed in the sky and the dew on the grass began to dry. It was early fall, and the morning hummed with bees and flies, mosquitoes and moths. Occasionally, birds flew overhead, roosters would crow, and every now and then, a bunny peeked out from the tall grass. The girls were dressed with their tied-up black-and-white oxfords and anklets, and jumpers with blouses or skirts and tops. Everyone's hair was brushed, combed, and braided into submission, with a big bow tied neatly on the side or at the nape. Legs and knees shone with Vaseline, Dixie Peach, or Jergens lotion to get the ashiness off the skin. Everyone carried a bag lunch or a lunch pail with a sandwich and fruit. The boys ran up in relays, picking and poking, pulling braids, and generally causing disruption. There were the Byrds: Bonnie and Gwen; the Mosses: Debbie, Barbara, and Ralph; the Brights: Cynthia and Jamesetta (cousins of the Byrds); the De Jarnettes: Harold Gene and Betty, who recently relocated from Virginia; the Smiths: Kenny and Wendell; Gwen Adams, the local beauty; Ruby Jean; and a number of other children, for a total of about thirty students.

Gradually, the children became aware of the sound of car tires on gravel, which could only mean one thing: Mrs. Dyson had arrived. Everyone stood back against the steps as the two-toned green Ford sedan pulled into place. As she exited the car, she said, "Good morning, children." "Good morning, Ms. Dyson," they replied in singsong unison.

Once Mrs. Dyson opened the doors, everyone formed a line, entered, hung up his or her sweater, and sat down at a desk with his or her lunch, hands folded neatly on top. Each row represented a grade: row one, first grade; row two, second grade; and so on through eighth grade. Bonnie was the only person in first grade. Next to her sat Debbie Moss, Ruby Jean, and Wendell Smith, the only second-graders. Third grade consisted of Gwen Byrd and Jamesetta Bright.

Mrs. Dyson maintained strict control of the classroom. She did most of the talking unless she posed a direct question to a student. She moved up and down the aisles, looking over assignments and directing the students' attention to assignments in other books and other workbooks.

On most occasions, the classroom atmosphere was fairly predictable, even boring. But certain events brought a flash of the outside world and beauty to the little school. Banking Day was such a day. On Banking Day, Wilmington Trust Bank sent a banking official to the school with a huge machine encased in glass. It was placed high on a table in the front of the classroom. The bank official spoke to the class about the importance of saving, and passed out savings books, in which the students were instructed to put their names. Every time the teller came, we were to bring at least one quarter, and he would put the quarter in the machine and crank the handle, and a stamp would come out to put into our hands, which we then licked and glued into our savings book. Few of us had quarters to put in the machine, but for those of us who did, it was a memorable event, and we looked forward to it.

The biggest celebration at State Line School was the May Day Program, which stretched from dawn to dusk and involved the whole Hickman Row community. At the event, everyone had costumes made of crepe paper. The girls were dressed to look like pastel-colored spring flowers with green stems and pink, yellow, or blue petals. We tied the maypole, danced, and sang. Our hair was pressed and curled. We twirled in our costumes like lilies in a pond, gently swaying in the warm summer evening, heavy with the scent of honeysuckle and moist, warm earth. All of our parents were present. The boys were dressed in their Sunday best with their shoes shined with Vaseline and Dixie Peach. We were the community's youth, and we were blooming and beautiful. Those who were graduates of the State Line School recalled their own maypole days as they sipped punch and ate cookies with tiny bites. Suddenly, we were all one and happy in this odd little corner of America, pleasantly absent from the oppression beyond The Row. As we walked toward our homes, that spring in 1957, none of us had an inkling of the massive sea change that was about to occur in our lives.

Summer passed slowly and lazily. Time was marked by the arrival of the *Weekly Reader* newspaper, to which Bonnie subscribed. It seemed to take no time to read the news stories about Israel and Russia. The crossword puzzle was even less taxing. But things were looking up. The Fourth of July was coming up and Union Baptist Church would be taking everyone on a picnic to Hersheypark.

Beily was going with the three children, who got new summer outfits in preparation, providing a uniform color code that would enable Beily to spot Bonnie, Boo, and Skip easily. The girls had to have their hair washed and straightened, which was at least a half-day ritual. Boo was what old folks referred to as "tender-headed"; she had fine light brown hair that had a curly, crinkly texture, and she hated to have it combed or brushed. Beily coaxed Boo into sitting between her knees as she began the age-old ritual between colored mommies and daughters... the combing of the hair. Gradually and gently, she combed out the tangles after washing Boo's hair and separated it into small balls. After carefully oiling each section, she reconsidered the task and braided her hair into two braids across the top and two in the back.

When it was Bonnie's turn, they had the same ritual, but Bonnie's hair had to be straightened with a hot comb, which meant risking fried ears and a burnt neck. But Beily and Bonnie persevered in the heat with a fan blowing and the stove burning until Bonnie's kinks were smooth and her bang curled across her face just like that of

Annette Funicello of the Mouseketeers. She was now presentable and ready for the trip.

On the Fourth of July morning, every family on Hickman Row was up and dressed, and had a picnic basket and a thermos of lemonade, ready to go. Children were antsy, and adults, happy to have a holiday. There was an air of anticipation and expectancy that hovered over The Row as palpable as the humidity in the air. That year, Richard had made arrangements for Union Baptist Church to be admitted to Hersheypark to enjoy the rides and the picnic facilities. It seems that even though Pennsylvania was a "free" northern state, Hersheypark had never before admitted a Negro group to enjoy the facilities. Union Baptist Church was the first Negro organization to gain admittance to the park.

A big yellow school bus rolled down Hickman Road and pulled in front of Union Baptist Church. Reverend Trotter, the superintendent of the Sunday school and chairman of the Deacon Board, organized everyone into a line and got everyone seated. Removing his hat, Deacon Trotter prayed for traveling mercies for the group. The door closed, and the bus lurched off toward the Pennsylvania line, which was less than five hundred feet from the church. During that time, every child on Hickman Row was told that many slaves had fled to freedom, risking their lives, crossing these same five hundred feet. Those who failed to escape into Pennsylvania ended up on the hanging tree at the opposite end of The Row at its juncture with Naamans Road. The tree stood like a tall, scarred black gargoyle at the entry of Dr. Wilson's property, down by the garage. Funny how the distance between heaven and hell could be as little as a few hundred yards.

Beily and Daisy had decided to drive up to the picnic together in Beily's navy blue wood-paneled Ford station wagon. The children were smooshed together on a pallet, along with all the baskets and thermoses, in the "way back," behind the second-row seat. These were the days of no air conditioning, so all the windows were rolled down and the children enjoyed the wind rushing through the windows. Beily and Daisy talked and cackled as only best girlfriends do. The children sang and clapped and made up games, making the time pass quickly.

Soon, they arrived at the entrance to Hersheypark. As the park was framed with a huge picture of a Hershey's Bar and chocolate kisses, the children knew that heaven was near. The park was surrounded by the wooden tracks of "The Thunderbolt," the famous roller coaster that had been known to make grown men weak in the knees after one zip around the park. The weathered gray wooden track rose and fell like a mountain range all around the park, and the click-click sound of the heavy chain that pulled the wooden roller coaster cars signaled the approaching roller coaster was about to begin the trek up a steep hill. Bonnie watched, fascinated, as the roller coaster rose high above their heads. As it approached the top, one brave soul lifted his arms and laughed. Others were holding the bar that held them in their seats for dear life. Slowly, the roller coaster reached the top. It stopped momentarily before cascading down the slope at breakneck speed with people screaming, "Ohhhh!'" Bonnie looked at Beily and said, "Can I go on that, Mommy?" "I don't think so, Bonnie," Beily replied. "You're my big girl, but not that big," she smiled. "C'mon, let's get some lunch." She and Daisy found a table and sat the children down for lunch. After spreading a red-and-white-checked cloth, they laid out fried chicken, potato salad, deviled eggs, potato chips, and fruit. Then, they poured sweet lemonade, thick with pulp and lemon slices, into waxed Dixie cups. Eager to get to the rides, the children ate quickly.

Bonnie had paired up with Debbie Moss and her father, Reuben, who had agreed to squire the two girls around the park. Beily and Daisy, along with Cliffie, Boo, and Skip, packed up home base and headed for the kiddie park. Beily and Daisy were the two most attractive women on Hickman Row. Daisy was small with a tiny waist and gently flared hips. She had a keen little nose, thin lips with a Cupid's bow arch, and small, lively brown eyes. When Daisy threw back her head and lifted her hands to laugh, you wanted to laugh too. She was lovely and fun and the closest friend Beily had ever had. Daisy and Beily treasured each other and their children. Clarence; Henry Jr., called "June"; and Barbara Ann, pronounced "Bar'bran," had ridden to the park on the bus to be with the big kids. They clambered up to Daisy to get their tickets, and as Daisy passed them out, she caressed each head and cheek, straightened their braids, and tugged shirts into place. She loved Henry and their children, and her pride showed as she gazed at the dusty wake her four eldest children left as they bounded off to catch up with friends. Bar'bran and Gwen sauntered off together, picking up Cynnie and Etta Bright as they moved toward the merry-go-round. Born leaders, Bar'bran and Gwen always stuck out in a positive way, much to their peers' chagrin. Nevertheless, they were all from The Row, and they stuck together like little clumps of dandelions in the mixed crowd of white Anglo-Saxon, protestant, Amish, and other colored people in Hersheypark that day.

Though it was hot and humid as only a July day in the Mid-Atlantic states can be, it was a beautiful day. Most everyone bought caramel popcorn, snowballs, cotton candy, chocolate bars, and ice cream. Firmly in most children's grips were pinwheels and hollow plastic canes filled with multicolored sugar beads. By the end of the afternoon, everyone returned to the pavilion hot, tired, and streaked with sweat and colored dyes from the snowballs they'd consumed throughout the day. Bonnie's hair – and everyone else's – had drawn up with the humidity, so her ponytails had become question marks and the Annette Funicello bang had become a close crop of kinky twists across the front of her head. Before leaving the park, she and the others rummaged through their picnic baskets for one more bite of a chicken wing and a swallow of lemonade.

Reverend Trotter had counted the heads to make sure everyone was ready to board the bus, but one person was missing. Ralph Moss, known as Ralphie, was somewhere in the park. Mr. Reuben had been sent to retrieve his errant son. Around the corner came Ralphie, looking devilish and sheepish with his big eyes, grin, and curly hair. Mr. Reuben walked behind, puffing from the exhaustion and chasing behind Ralphie. "Let's load up," Deacon Trotter said.

The yellow bus loaded and pulled off, heading toward home. Beily and Daisy followed. The children were quiet, as it had been a busy day for them. Cliffie and Skipper slept on the second seat. Boo slept in the way back with Bonnie, who lay awake watching the evening give way to dusk, listening to her momma and her auntie talk just above The Platters singing "I Only Have Eyes for You." The car swayed gently back and forth, lulling her into a peaceful sleep.

Chapter 14

DESEGREGATION COMES TO CLAYMONT

In the next school year, starting September 1957, Claymont Public Education decided it was time to desegregate the elementary grades. In 1952, the high schools had been desegregated without much publicly, recorded notice or fanfare – although many of the participants had stories of abuse and mistreatment never shared or uttered to shield their parents from fear.

Bernice Byrd, Bonnie's older cousin and Roosevelt's daughter, had been a key participant in that event. "Sandy," as Bernice was nicknamed because of her light, hazel eyes, was a brilliant student, quick of mind and speech. She had been relinquished by her mother, "Fatty," and raised by her grandparents Lee and Sarah. Roosevelt also lived with them, having returned from World War II mentally broken and damaged beyond repair. General George S. Patton and Field Marshal Erwin Rommel had been too much for this gentle soul to withstand. Roosevelt returned home quiet, withdrawn, and fragile, completely unlike the outgoing ladies' man that had left Hickman Row for the war. The best sight Richard said he ever saw was his brother coming over the hill, home to Hickman Row and his family. Roosevelt came home, crawled into a liquor bottle, and pulled the cork on top, tightly closing in his abilities, hopes, aspirations, and dreams, along with whatever demons he brought home from the war. It was all closed inside of dear Roosevelt, never to be shared again. Gramma and Grandpop kept his bedroom available, and somehow Rokie always managed to get home to sleep. Occasionally, he and Grandpop erupted in a threatening drunken rage, but more often than not, everything operated with a slight buzz of gin or whiskey to soften the memories, the demons, and the constant rejection and fear that accompanied being a colored person living in a segregated southern town.

In September 1957, the elementary schoolchildren lined up at the Union Hall, waiting for the bus to Green Street Elementary, the white school. The high school students had been picked up already; that was fairly well established over the past couple of years. However, it was a new thing for the elementary kids to be sent out of the protective arms and extended family of Hickman Row. Here everyone was an auntie or an uncle. You were always somebody's baby. The world beyond was quite a bit different, though. Oddly enough, none of the adults spoke to the children in preparation for the change. The only sign that something was afoot was the women stood on the porches to watch the children board the bus. They stood silently and fearful, consoling one another as the bus pulled ahead and disappeared down the hill, trusting God and prayer to keep them safe from harm and hateful white people.

As the bus drove away from Hickman Row and turned onto Naamans Road, the children sat quietly. The only time they had ridden a school bus was when Mrs. Dyson took them on field trips or to perform for local leadership at the Episcopal Church of the Ascension, where they sang, *"Mama's little baby loves short'nin' bread."* But this trip was different, and the children, feeling the welling tension, sat still and silent, gripping their brown lunch bags and colorful lunch pails.

As the bus pulled into the broad driveway of the school, the children saw it was choked with angry-looking white people milling about. The driver, an old, wizened white man named Ray in round horn-rimmed spectacles, a straw hat, a worn plaid shirt, and overalls, eased the bus through the people, pulling up to the school entrance. Wordlessly, he opened the door to the bus. Nobody moved. The children sat frozen in their seats, afraid of the angry white people swirling around the school entrance and approaching the windows. Mr. Ray turned around in his seat to face us. "Well, go on," he drawled. "Get on to school." Bonnie didn't know who stood up first, but somehow they stumbled down the steps and off the bus.

They each had a slip of white paper with a room number and a teacher's name written on it. Somehow Bonnie found her classroom, 109, and her teacher, Ms. Boggs. She was tall and slender with poppy brown eyes and brunette hair worn in a tightly curled neck-length pageboy reminiscent of Rosemary Clooney. Her uncle was Caleb Boggs, Delaware's U.S. senator, and she had recently been crowned Miss Delaware as a participant in the Miss America contest. Ms. Boggs was not unkind, but rather distant, matter-of-fact, and efficient in her mannerisms. She showed Bonnie where to sit. As she sat, she caught a glimpse of the boy who would sit behind her. He was sticking out his tongue at her and making horrid faces. Bonnie slid into her chair. Suddenly, she felt someone pull her braids hard. She turned around to face the mean boy again, who was sticking his tongue out at her. He muttered, "You n'een yer"; "you n'een yer." "Billy, be quiet," Ms. Boggs said.

Ms. Boggs stepped to the front of the class. "Good morning, children, and welcome to second grade." Billy was still muttering behind her, but Bonnie leaned forward to keep him from pulling her braids. She looked around slowly to observe the rest of the room. It was about half the size of her class at State Line School. Nobody had braids or brown skin, and nobody smiled. *I don't think I'm going to like it here*, Bonnie thought. Soon it was time for recess. Ms. Boggs lined the children up at the back door, and everyone ran out to play. Bonnie sauntered out of the door and just stood to look around. "Chocolate, chocolate baby," she could hear some of her classmates chanting. It seemed no one wanted to play, so Bonnie contented herself near the door. "Go play," Ms. Boggs urged her. *But with whom?*

Bonnie thought. As she turned toward the playground, a couple of boys ran by and hit her with pebbles. Before she could see who they were, they'd run off. Surely, Ms. Boggs had to have seen who had done that. She was standing right next to her. But Ms. Boggs' back was turned, and she seemed unaware of Bonnie's presence.

"Recess is over, children. Line up." The children ran toward the door. Some of them kicked and punched her as they ran past. "N'een yer, n'een yer," Billy said, smiling a toothless, mean grimace. *This is not a happy place*, Bonnie thought, a*nd what is a n'een yer? Why do they call me chocolate?*

Somehow Bonnie got through the day and on the bus to go home. All the children were silent and numb on the bus ride. *I guess their days were miserable, too*, Bonnie thought.

When Beily came to pick up Bonnie, her sister, and her brother from Daisy's that evening, she glanced anxiously at Bonnie. "Did you have a good day?" she asked. "No, I didn't, Mommy. They hit me and scratched me and called me n'een yer and chocolate. Why are they so mean to me?"

"Oh, baby, chocolate is sweet. They like you."

"No, they don't. I don't want to go there. Please don't make me go."

"You have to go to school, baby. It will be all right."

Richard heard Bonnie recount the story at home. Frustrated, he kept silent and paced between the kitchen and the living room, punching his opposite palm. "It never ends," he said. "Never." Richard grabbed a coat and slammed out of the house.

The next morning, the same scene played out, except this time Bonnie and the others braced themselves for the assault. They exited the bus like little soldiers performing a drill, quickly moving to the classroom, eager to get the day over with. The dreaded recess hour recurred, with the same experience that Bonnie had endured before.

Later that afternoon on the bus, Gwen and Etta sat in the seats in front of and behind Bonnie's. "Are you getting beat up?" Etta asked in the direct, pointed way she had of speaking. "Well, yeah, I guess so," Bonnie said. "Yeah, she's getting beat up," Gwen said. "Look at her clothes." "We'll just have to do sumpthin' about it." Bonnie looked from one cousin to the other. She wasn't sure what they were up to, but one thing was for sure: Etta would sooner beat you down than talk to you, and the resolve in Gwen's words meant something was going to happen. What was a little kid to do?

The next day, Bonnie was antsy. Once on the bus, Gwen and Etta assumed their seats. "Don't worry about a thing," they said, and walked off the bus toward their classrooms. When recess time came, Bonnie stepped out onto the playground as usual. Keeping her back to the wall, she figured she would brace her back and easily spy anyone or anything coming from the other three angles. Suddenly, coming straight at her were two girls kicking up dust toward her and throwing handfuls of dust. Coughing and shielding her face, Bonnie turned to see her two cousins, Gwen and Etta, just out from the classroom next door, beginning to kick and throw dirt back at the girls. In a split second, teachers came from everywhere, and before they knew it, all of them, Negro and white, had been swept into the vice principal's office. Mr. Lipka was a tall, stately white man with steel gray hair and sparkly blue eyes. "Girls," he said, "this is not how Green Street Elementary School is going to work. We are going to be friends, and we are going to get along. It's going to start now." He made us all shake hands, and he gave us each a butterscotch toffee. As we left his office, he said, "Don't come back here like this ever again, girls. Not ever again."

With that, they each sauntered off to the classroom. At the turn in the hallway, Bonnie said good-bye to Gwen and Etta. "Thanks, guys. Sorry you got in trouble." "S'okay, cuz. Sometimes ya just gotta fight," Etta said. "C'mon girl," Gwen said. "We're already in enough stuff."

Gwen and Etta disappeared down the hall, leaving Bonnie alone in the hallway with the two white girls with whom she'd been fighting. She knew their names from class: Karen Hallburg, who was tough like a tomboy, with chin-length, white blond hair with a cowlick, blue eyes, and freckles; and Christine Blair, a thin, tan girl with freckles and short brown hair. "We'd like to be friends," Christine said. "Whew, me too," said Karen. "We were just acting up. Sorry." Pausing for a moment to think about how mean the girls had been and her dad's anger, Bonnie weighed the options. Clearly, someone had to forgive, and at least Chris had offered first. Bonnie replied, "Yes, I want to be friends, too." "Great!" said Karen. By that time, they had reached the classroom door. The girls slipped into their seats quietly. Ms. Boggs didn't seem to take notice of their presence. After Bonnie sat down, Billy yanked her braid. She turned around and smashed Billy's nose good and hard. He appeared to be genuinely shocked that she had landed a good one on his squat, ugly nose. Bonnie was tired of the boy's taunts, and Mr. Lipka wasn't there to help. Interestingly enough, despite Billy's cries, Ms. Boggs never turned around or seemed to notice there was any disruption. Maybe she had decided they would work it out. "Leave her alone," Bonnie heard. "Yeah, leave her alone, Billy, or you'll have to deal with us." Bonnie turned around to see Chris and Karen smiling and winking. "Yeah," Bonnie said. "You'll have to deal with us." Billy visibly shrank and looked confused... and that was the last time he made fun of Bonnie.

Later that afternoon, on the ride home from school, Bonnie noticed Mr. Hawkins was not taking the usual route back to Hickman Row. In fact, he had pulled off the Philadelphia Pike and was riding out of the way down Naamans Road to a desolate area, where he pulled onto an unpaved roadway. Most of the children knew this road led to White's Village, a mobile home community for poor whites that was not frequented by colored folks. At this point, the eight or so of them on the bus were alarmed. Mr. Hawkins pulled the bus over and turned the ignition off. He turned to them, his red, swarthy, sweating face looking mean and hard. He pushed the brim of his sweat-stained gray hat back from his face, pulled out a filthy handkerchief, and wiped his continuously sweating brow. He rose from the driver's seat and began to pace the aisle. "Now, which one of you kids said I was calling you niggers?" he said. No one moved. No one said a word. "Someone said one of y'all had told Mr. Lipka I called you niggers," he said, stopping and bending down to peer into our eyes. We remained still and silent. "You know I could drive you back here and lose you," he said with an evil cackle. "Never see your parents again." He walked toward his seat slowly, started up the engine, and turned the bus around. The kids were never so glad to see Hickman Row and practically knocked one another over trying to get off the bus.

No one ever discussed that incident or that day. Being part of a desegregation plan was not fun.

The rest of the year was a piece of cake. Bonnie did well in school, so well that the school tested her intelligence and wanted her to skip a couple of grades. After evaluating the situation, Richard said: "No. She's going through enough. Let her be."

As time passed, Bonnie found her way through the intertwined emotions, actions, and social behaviors involved with integration Claymont-style. She became a Brownie and was comfortable navigating between life on Hickman Row and her friends who lived in Darley Woods. They exchanged visits at one another's homes and just plain had fun the way kids do when they're left without the political/cultural influences of their elders.

As good as things had gotten for Bonnie, that's how unhappy they'd grown for Beily and Richard. Love and longing were not enough to keep a family together. Unexplained absences and annual trips to England had made it difficult for Beily to hang on, and Richard did not understand his wife's desire to belong to Wilmington's phony, brittle Negro middle class. He was uncomfortable with small talk and the double entendre so common among them. War and death had left him little desire to play games with people. He had been too close to the real in life... real blood and real death. The chasm between them had grown to a point where neither could cross it. So one clear fall day in 1960, Beily packed up the house, and she and the children moved back to 301. The children were numb, and so was Beily. She loved Richard, but she could not live with him with his bouts of depression and anger, behavior that would later come to be identified as post-traumatic stress disorder. It was hard on her and the children. Once again, 301 became a refuge and a haven for Beily and the children. This time, the transition would be permanent. The move took all of her strength, and she knew she could never muster it again. So Beily marched forward with resolve and never looked back, leaving Richard and the children to establish communication and maintain relationship across the deep flesh and spirit gorge between them.

Chapter 15

SO LONG, BAD HAIR DAYS

Growing up, Bonnie's hair had always been a challenge for her, as for most black women, and the comparison between her and other girls, and later women, began. Her momma always had beautiful hair, a pretty auburn brown color worn below her shoulders with a big pompadour in the front. Sometimes she'd even put a blond streak in the back. Bonnie's dad always said he never knew where Bonnie had gotten her hair. As a baby, she had cradle cap, or a flaky scalp with short little kinks. Her mom kept it all under those cute little caps that babies wore in the 1950s until one of her mean colleagues snatched one off. Beily patiently oiled and brushed and braided it until Bonnie's hair gradually grew in, thick and kinky, but long enough for three braids that reached her shoulders. Eventually, Bonnie learned to care for her hair mostly on her own, except for the every-other-week ritual of wash, dry, and comb press, which she dreaded. This process involved a lot of discomfort and sometimes outright pain. Combing out wet hair required sectioning her hair with a comb and then pulling through the kinks. Beily was usually pretty careful, so Bonnie could get through that. But then the little balls of combed-out hair had to dry out and be oiled and pressed with the hot comb. If the hair wasn't dry, steam was created close to the scalp, which was painful. Because her hair was thick, it took a long time to dry, especially close to the scalp. So Bonnie frequently had the steam burn.

Eventually, Beily wanted to find another way to take care of Bonnie's hair. So on a beautiful Saturday morning, she took Bonnie to her own renowned hair salon in Philadelphia, Ace and Ada's, to get a permanent straightener in her hair as a "growing up" treat. Bonnie was ten years old, and at that awkward stage, she was prepubescent and slightly chubby. Little girls clothes were too snug, and preteen clothing was too big... so Bonnie was relegated to the purgatory of the children's department, the "chubby" section. Because her parents had recently separated, her world was already upside down. She'd moved from the country to the city, from a small elementary school where she was in the brainiac section to a large urban elementary school where she was placed in the slow performers and bad behavior section, better known by her teacher, Mrs. Neubauer, as the maniacs. Bonnie's mom had grown very thin with worry about bills and adjusting to unmarried life. Beily was a stressed mess. From Bonnie's perspective, their relationship was more like big peer and little peer than mother and child, and Bonnie knew her mommy was close to the cracking point. But this was one day away in the big city for fun and beauty. It was going to be carefree. Great!

Ace and Ada's was a sophisticated salon. There were nicely appointed antique white and gold chairs, a beautiful white leather sofa, and a glass coffee table with magazines. The receptionist offered coffee or tea while people waited for their hairdresser to take them behind the door leading from the reception area to the salon. Sitting beside her mother on the sofa, Bonnie looked into the mirror on the wall across from where they were seated.

Bonnie thought Beily was the prettiest woman in the room. Other women looked at her and nodded and smiled. Bonnie looked at her own reflection somewhat ruefully. One section of hair on top of her head was combed to the left and double strand-twisted, sealed at the end with a barrette that fell to the top of her shoulder. The rest of her hair was gathered into a ponytail that twist-curled in a similar fashion and hung to the center of her back. It, too, was sealed with a silver barrette.

Bonnie could hear women talking and laughing behind the door that led to the salon. Hair dryers hummed, and occasionally you would get a whiff of something strong, pungent, and acidic, similar to burnt eggshells. A small brown-skinned woman with a blue smock appeared at the door. "Mrs. Byrd and Bonnie?" she stated. Then she recognized Bonnie's mother. "Hi, Beily," she said, smiling. "And this must be Bonnie. Come on back."

Once in the salon, Bonnie felt like she'd crossed over from the children's playground to womanhood. This was a place of serious business. Visages were transformed – eyebrows were arched; hairy lips and chins, de-fuzzed. Fingernails and toenails were being painted every color of the rainbow. Kinky hair was made slick with a foul-smelling white cream, which then was rinsed from the hair, and the silky, straight strands were shampooed. The clean, damp hair was combed through with a green slimy setting lotion, rolled with an end paper on a wire-mesh roller, and clipped into place with pin clips. Rollers were placed in a particular pattern, depending on the look the hairdresser was trying to achieve. For instance, some rollers were turned up for a flip or a French roll. The process was truly an art. You had to select the right size roller for the right size curl and to fit the particular space on the patron's head. The salon also sold wigs, jewelry, handbags, and scarves. Cleopatra wigs in every color were the rage, along with braids, buns, and ponytails.

Nobody gave Bonnie as much as a second glance as she walked over to the chair Dorothy indicated. Bonnie listened as her mother explained that she wanted a perm for her hair because it was becoming too much for her to handle. As Dorothy unplaited Bonnie's braids, she exclaimed over the thickness and the length, "Yeah, girl, I can see you'd have your hands full dealin' with this!"

"Now, Dorothy, just remember, Bonnie's hair looks like it requires a lot of heat to straighten it, but it doesn't take much. I just use a warm comb, and it lays quite nicely," Beily said.

"Okay, girl, I gotcha," Dorothy said.

81

With that said, she urged Bonnie to sit up straight while she put the neck paper around Bonnie's throat and tied the cape snuggly over it. Bonnie could hear Dorothy, often referred to as Dottie, chewing gum quickly and thoughtfully as she combed her hair and sectioned it from forehead to nape. Starting at the nape, she applied the foul-smelling white cream along the roots of Bonnie's hair, working it through to the ends. Gradually, Dottie had applied the cream over Bonnie's entire head and began combing the cream through the hair. By then, Bonnie's scalp was tingling uncomfortably, and the smell was pretty acrid.

"Better let it set a minute," Dottie said.

Bonnie looked at her mother, but remained quiet. After a bit, she said: "It doesn't feel good. I want to get it out of my hair." Dottie had returned and said, "Okay, let's rinse." Bonnie quickly moved to a line of five shampoo bowls, four of which patrons and hairdressers occupied. Water flushing and shampoo sudsing were happening everywhere. She sat down and arched her back, sitting as high in the seat as she could. She wanted

that stuff off her head in the worst way, and the sooner the better. Dorothy turned on the water.

"If it's too cool, baby, let me know, but this will soothe your scalp," she murmured.

Despite her city slang, there was a soft drawl to her words reminiscent of her southern roots. Dorothy rinsed Bonnie's hair, starting at the hair around the face, then moving through the crown and down the back of Bonnie's head. She lifted Bonnie's head and rinsed the back of it and her nape. Suddenly, she turned the water off. "Ann! Ann!" she cried. "Come here."

A smallish older woman came over. She looked in the bowl and looked at Dottie. "I'll get Beily," she said, and walked quickly away. No one looked at Bonnie or seemed to be aware of her existence. Though it was her head in the bowl, no one was talking to her about the obvious calamity. By then, Bonnie knew something, and something not so good, was up. Ann returned with Beily, who looked into the bowl and fainted dead away. Bonnie got up from her chair. "Mommy, Mommy, are you all right? Help my mommy!" she said calmly, but firmly, looking from Ann to Dottie. Bonnie reached for her mother's hand, patting it until the color reappeared in her cheeks. Ann and Dottie helped Beily into a chair. Someone rushed over with a glass of cold water and a cool cloth. By then, it seemed the whole salon was focused on Beily and the bowl. After Beily came around, she said, "Bonnie, your hair is broken off in the back. It'll have to be cut and styled."

"How much is broken off?" Bonnie asked.

"Down to the scalp, I'm afraid. Oh, honey, I'm sooo sorry," Beily said, and she started to cry.

"Mommy, Mommy, don't cry," Bonnie said. "It's only hair, not brain cells. Besides, I want to look like a big girl, and it'll grow. You'll see."

"Yes, yes, of course," Beily said. "It will grow... and we'll take very good care of it."

Gingerly, Bonnie reached for the back of her head. The right side seemed fine, but the left side was as bald as a peach from below the ear to the nape. There was no length to the hair above this spot to midway up the crown. The hair at her crown was thin and felt weak. Bonnie really wanted to cry. She wanted to bawl and scream and hit Dottie and Ann and pick her hair up out of the bowl and paste it back on her head. She wanted time to roll back forty-five minutes to before this happened. But it wasn't forty-five minutes earlier. Bonnie was partially bald, Beily was distraught, and they were in a strange place surrounded by people who clearly didn't act out like that. Bonnie had to hold it together… and she did. "Could you show me some styles that I might consider?" Bonnie asked. Dottie turned to look at Bonnie with a combination of wonder and gratefulness. Looking back, Bonnie realized Dottie must have been in her late teens or early twenties, and was probably still in training. After that, perhaps her job was even in jeopardy.

"Sure," Dottie said. She handed Bonnie Seventeen and *American Girl* magazines, both targeting the Caucasian population, with their fixation on teased page boys à la Jackie Kennedy certainly not applicable to a little Negro girl who found herself suddenly partially bald. But Bonnie's optimism and pluck kicked in, and she found a picture of a popular haircut, a pixie, she thought might work, given the remaining hair on her head.

"I think a pixie cut would suit you fine, and I can shingle the back to cover this area where it's thin," Dottie said.

"Okay," Bonnie said. "Let's get busy. My momma needs to see me looking pretty."

Dottie finished Bonnie's haircut, rolled it, and sat her under the dryer. About thirty minutes later, Bonnie was declared done. Dottie took the rollers out, brushed and combed, teased and sprayed. She handed the mirror to Bonnie. "It's nice," she said, "and I can barely see the bald spot." "There's no charge, of course." Beily and Bonnie drove home silently.

When Bonnie got home, her sister and her friends, Dottie Talbert and Ann Turner, greeted her. They all still had their braids, and during that time, no sane Negro female who could grow hair ever cut it voluntarily. They knew something horrible had happened. Mercifully, they just stared at Bonnie with their mouths open, and then returned their attention to their dolls. Bonnie ran upstairs to the bathroom, shut the door, and turned on the water. She cried and cried until her nose got red and ran. She looked in the mirror and thought that was the ugliest she had ever looked. "Please, God, let my hair grow," she prayed.

Though that incident was more than forty years ago – and since then, Bonnie's hair has been fried, dyed, and laid on the side – the sting of unexpectedly losing her hair due to chemical damage has never quite left her. Recently, Bonnie decided to return her hair to its natural texture, as she was sick of the bondage she felt about going to a hair salon. She longed for the look and freedom of just enjoying her hair as it was without a straightener. But she didn't want to be gray, so she dyed it, and she wanted to loosen the kink a bit, so she texturized it. Yikes! Gadzooks! She'd double-processed her hair! The predictable result was that it broke off down to the quick. Bonnie awakened one morning with a mohawk, and hair was lying on the pillow. She sneaked out of bed quietly, called a dear friend, Vinnie Sorden, explained her personal tragedy, and begged for her to help her before her husband awakened and found her in that state. Like Zorro, Vinnie arrived in the nick of time and calmly drove Bonnie to her hair salon, where she got a TWA, a teeny-weeny Afro. When she got home and touched her hair, she was ten years old again at Ace and Ada's, trying not to cry. However, with some earrings, eye makeup, and swagger, it wasn't so bad, and thank God, hair does grow. Unlike Bonnie's first incident, though, this time she got scads of compliments from family and strangers alike. Bonnie guessed she'd finally grown into who she really was. Best of all, as a neighbor friend of hers who also sports a sharp TWA commented, "There are no bad hair days."

Chapter 16

BACK TO 301

Returning to 301 North Cleveland, Bonnie felt both happy and anxious. She was in a new school that she hated. In Claymont, she had reached the nirvana of the fifth grade: Ms. Reagan's class. She was a former nun who taught Spanish. Everyone loved her and wanted to be in her class, and Bonnie was one of the lucky ones. She had begun learning and practicing Spanish at home. All of her good buddies from her Brownie troop were in that class, and she was riding high.

Lore School, her new elementary school in Wilmington, was anything but pleasant. Bonnie was in the mentally slow fifth-grade class, and they were learning subjects she'd covered in second grade. Her classmates were not engaging, and were always fighting and hitting one another. Bonnie didn't understand their behavior, so she kept her distance.

She had made one friend, Shelly Warren. Shelly, who played the cello, lived with her grandmother not far from the school. The two girls became fond companions during a time when Bonnie needed one. She was experiencing anxiety in getting adjusted to city life again and due to her hair falling out. She was on constant alert to make sure the bald spot was covered at all times, and Shelly was her "bald spot checker." Bonnie would ask throughout the day, "Shelly, can you see my bald spot?" And Shelly would reply, "Oh, yeah, Bonita, I can see it... and it's turrible, just turrible!"

Somehow Bonnie made it through the school year and adjusted to being back at 301. The neighborhood had changed. New families had moved in; the Whites and the Porters were of particular interest.

They had daughters a year older than Bonnie named Elaine and Marilyn. The three had played softball for the Park League over the summer and hung out at Mack Park. Just as Bonnie thought they might be able to develop a relationship, they were off to junior high school at Bayard, but she was in sixth grade, still at Lore School. Bonnie's original chums, Mary Lou and Lee, had started attending Dunleith Elementary, where their mother, Mrs. Hannah Johnson, taught school, so they were rarely in the area. Bonnie spent the next couple of years exploring the neighborhood for friends, meeting the new neighbors, and participating in extracurricular activities. It was an unhappy, uncomfortable time.

In sixth grade, Bonnie returned to the top academic class. Mrs. McGordy taught the gifted and talented sixth-grade class, and she did not like "colored" children. She treated Bonnie with what could best be described as "benign neglect." She didn't try to hurt Bonnie, but she sure didn't want to help her. She never recognized her hand when it was raised and never included Bonnie in special opportunities, but Bonnie's grades remained outstanding. Beily's joy at her daughter's academic success was enough to keep Bonnie focused on achieving. Just seeing her mother smile and hearing her say, "Bonnie, you are being a good leader for your sister and brother to follow" was reward enough.

Bonnie breezed through sixth grade and entered Bayard Junior High School. Her guidance counselor, Anthony Carfagnol, was a wonderfully funny man who was always egging her on to take the most challenging courses. At this level, all students were tracked academically according to IQ and academic performance. These were the students Bonnie would compete against for the balance of her academic career in public school.

Bonnie's seventh-grade class was an interesting slice of Americana... English, Polish, Lithuanian, Italian, Negro, Jewish, and Asian. As an academic group, they were Seventh Grade, Group One.

Fortunately, they grew to be much more than a number. They played sports together, partied together, competed together, and grew into young adulthood together. They taught one another to dance, visited one another's homes after school, ate the delicacies from one another's homes, studied together, and just hung out together. They learned they were all human, loving, laughing, and seeking the same things – life, liberty, and the pursuit of happiness, as trite as that may sound today.

Some of the best split pea soup Bonnie ever had the pleasure of eating was at Barbara Chin's home. Her parents were pleasant, welcoming entrepreneurs who operated a laundry on Fourth Street. Barbara had a handsome brother named Harry and a gorgeous sister, Louise, who married a good-looking Italian from New York City. When Louise got married, the reception was held at the finest Asian restaurant on Delaware Avenue in Wilmington. The place settings were porcelain, and the utensils were solid ivory. It was a beautiful, upscale affair, and Bonnie was fortunate to have been invited. Mr. and Mrs. Chin were so proud and happy. Barbara wore the latest hairstyle, an asymmetrical bob, courtesy of Louise, and she was dressed in the finest mod outfit, the height of fashion, à la Rudi Gernreich, that could be found in the early 1960s. Louise was the most beautiful bride Bonnie had ever seen, in a full-length white gown that was straight out of *Vogue* magazine.

Barbara, Linda Hunt, Sharon Finnegan, and Bonnie were the preteens who observed it all. The four of them had become fast friends early in the process of becoming junior high students. They called themselves "The United Nations" because their nationalities reflected the world. They joined Girl Scouts together, and later, orchestra and various and sundry other school organizations.

On November 22, 1963, The Harvest Ball was held at school. It was the first dress-up dance for the school year, and all the students were excited. The school had elected a Harvest Ball Court, and the seventh grade had elected representatives for the court: Linda Pepeta and Wyvette Wade, the most beautiful and popular class members. The girls had purchased semiformal dresses, and the guys were to wear suits. It was all very exciting and grown up.

That afternoon, Bonnie and several of the other kids who were Student Council representatives busied themselves in the gym hanging decorations in preparation for the evening. They placed bales of hay and arranged pumpkins around the gym to create a fall scene. They stuffed scarecrows. They hung colored corn on the walls. The air was festive, and they practiced dance steps in anticipation of a lovely evening.

Suddenly, Mrs. Naughton, the gym teacher, swung the door open. She looked disheveled, dazed, and a bit frightened. The intercom system beeped in preparation for an announcement. "Attention, please! Attention, please! There is an emergency announcement!" It was the familiar voice of Mr. Young, the vice principal, but he sounded different, stressed, choked up. Everyone immediately sensed that something monumental was very wrong. All eyes swung up to look at the brown box that was placed squarely under the clock at the front of the gym. "President Kennedy has been assassinated in Dallas, Texas. I repeat, President Kennedy has been assassinated in Dallas, Texas." At this point in the message, Mr. Young's voice cracked audibly. All student activities for the evening are canceled. Students are dismissed immediately. I repeat, all student activities for the evening are canceled. There is no Harvest Ball."

For a moment, the students all stood there in the gym stunned in silence. Carol Woolfolk shrieked and ran to the girls lavatory. Others followed. A number of those present just stood there, trying to comprehend what it meant for the president to be assassinated. What about Mrs. Kennedy? What about Caroline and John-John? Were we at war? Was this the Bay of Pigs again? Why would anyone want to kill the president? Should we be prepared for a nuclear attack?

Hurriedly, Barbara, Linda, Sharon, and Bonnie gathered their books. They stopped by Mr. Carfagnol's office, their anchor away from home. He was reassuring and kind, urging us to get home quickly and turn on Walter Cronkite to get the latest, most accurate account of the events. They hustled home as quickly as possible, confused, sad, and anxious. This event was not part of our understanding of America. We were kids of the Sputnik Era. The Communists were our enemy. We had to be ready to go to the moon. Isn't that why we were studying SMSA math and science, and working out to "Go You Chicken Fat Go Away"? Wasn't the enemy over there in Russia?

When Bonnie arrived at home that afternoon, Boo, Skip, and Beily were already there huddled around the television, listening to Mr. Cronkite's version of the assassination of President Kennedy. The president was special in most Negro homes because of what we hoped he would do for our people – end segregation, help us attain equality as men and women in American society. We were aware of his discussions with Dr. King and the fact that his concerns about Negroes did not sit well with a lot of the southern members of the Democratic Party.

As we huddled around the television for the latest news, we watched as Lee Harvey Oswald was walked down the hall for his arraignment. Suddenly, shots rang out. He was murdered live in front of our very eyes on national television. Later, an elderly white man, Jack Ruby, was caught and jailed as the responsible party. All of this was disconcerting. Beily turned off the television and turned on the recordings they had of the Fisk Jubilee Singers. The soloist sang a mournful "Nobody Knows the Trouble I've Seen." We all felt sad and a bit scared.

Bonnie spoke with her dad that evening on the telephone to get his take on the situation. They were afraid. Was this a plot of the Communists? If things got that shaky, they would have to go to Claymont and stay in the fallout shelter her dad had built in the basement of the house. Nope, according to her dad, this was Cholly once again. A lot of people in high and powerful places were invested in us Negroes remaining as close to slaves as possible. Cheap or dang near free Negro labor was the key to the U.S. economy. Yes, this was just another manifestation of white folks and their efforts to keep us in bondage.

Bonnie never conceived that Cholly spread his tent so broad and wide as to encompass the control of the presidency of our country. It gave her pause, and for the first time, Bonnie began to see that the direction of one's life was not always shaped positively by birth into a wealthy family like the ones who employed Nana, or even hard work and study, or academic prowess. While power and privilege had their advantages, sometimes evil showed up and trumped everything. The aftermath of the evil that was perpetrated on President Kennedy and its impact on her life and the whole post-war generation of youths would reverberate for many years to come.

One day at the end of ninth grade, Bonnie received a call to come to the principal's office. She was invited to attend a dinner sponsored by the GOP, where she would be recognized as the highest academic performer in the graduating class at Bayard Junior High School. The dinner was held at the Hotel duPont, in the Gold Ballroom, a very tony kind of landmark in the city, and Bonnie was given a gold medal inscribed with her name in recognition of her academic achievement.

In many ways, it was a defining moment for Bonnie. Academic performance became the way through which she decided to rise to significance. She wasn't pretty like her momma, but she was smart like her dad. It made both of her parents and Nana very happy. Academic achievement seemed to open doors to special opportunities. This was her identified and chosen way forward to the future she planned to have. Her mother and father were constantly telling her: "Get an education. Get all you can. That and Jesus are the only things they (white folks) cannot take away from you." Everything her mom and dad and Nana had taught her thus far supported this simple truth. Bonnie was determined to do her best to invest everything in her to obtain the best education possible for her and for them.

Chapter 17

THE MYSTERIOUS PLACE NEXT DOOR

While "The Little Acre" at 301 was at the corner of Third Street and Cleveland Avenue, on the West Side of Wilmington, on the corner of Fourth Street and Cleveland Avenue stood a lovely, well-crafted brick house that was the proud home of Mr. and Mrs. Echols Young, their only child and pride and joy, Thelma Ellen, and, for a time, Mr. Young's niece, Amy. Mrs. Young was a teacher or administrator, as I recall, a short, stout woman with large round eyes. She wore her hair pulled up in the back into a kind of cornucopia of curls that cascaded over her brow. Because she was short, she seemed to always peer upward, which caused her to lift her brows. As a result, Mrs. Young always appeared quizzical, as though she had a question on the tip of her tongue to ask you but somehow never got around to it. She had a somewhat stern, no-nonsense appearance that older Negro women cultivated then: practical dark shoes with an oxford front, laced and tied with black shoelaces, and solid, square heels about two inches tall, suitable for support and walking. Her hose was dark and opaque. Her clothing was of a like manner: dark, nondescript, and covering every square inch of her body from throat to ankle. She would never be described as stylish, but she was certainly appropriate and formidable. It was the armor many Negro women wore then as protection against the image of the oversexed, wanton, uneducated woman who was easy pickin's. Truly, Mrs. Young was the antithesis of that woman. In fact, there had to have been at least three layers of snuggies and underwear and foundations holding everything together under her dress. Nothing and no one was getting into Mrs. Young's armor. Nope. No body. Not even the wind!

Mrs. Young spoke clear, crisp English and tolerated no other standard in her home from Thelma Ellen. Speaking of her daughter, oddly, everyone in the neighborhood referred to Thelma Ellen by both of her names, spoken clearly and distinctly together in the same breath. Even if Mrs. Young was in a hurry, she would call, "Thelm'ellen!" But on most occasions, the two distinct names were spoken separately.

During her travels in the neighborhood, Bonnie observed that not many people visited the Youngs' home, except her and maybe the paper boy to collect his weekly payment. Even then, she didn't think anyone ever entered the house beyond the sunporch. *She* certainly had gotten only as far as the sunporch, peering into the foyer, and Mrs. Young always stood in the middle of the doorway, so you couldn't see around her, which was pretty odd. No one else in the neighborhood behaved like that except, well, the Youngs. However, they were unique and entitled to their privacy and freedom from her curiosity. Even when Bonnie was selling Girl Scout cookies, she wasn't invited inside. But it was clear that Mrs. Young ran the inside of that home much as an army sergeant ran his troops.

Thelma Ellen did not attend the public schools in the area, and she didn't play with any of the kids in the neighborhood. She never even came outside to play. Every now and then, Bonnie caught a glimpse of her in the backseat of her parents' car, driving away to some unknown place. And then one day, she went away to college. The word in the neighborhood was that she graduated from Morgan State University in Baltimore, Maryland, a highly respected historically black college. Not long after that, Bonnie saw her with a tall, handsome brown-skinned man with a pipe, and it seemed they were married. After that, Thelma Ellen never came back.

Nevertheless, the most interesting person in the family was Mr. Young. Even his name, Echols, was unique. Mr. Young was a cook at the Walnut Street Y, the social and political hub of the Negro community in Wilmington then. He cooked at the counter for local patrons grabbing a quick bite, for social organizations raising funds, and for visiting dignitaries who required special dainties. Echols was the chef in charge at the Y. But when Echols came home, he retreated to his garden. It was his refuge from people both at work and at home. The minute he pulled the car into the garage and the missus and Thelma Ellen exited the house and ascended its brick steps, you could count on Mr. Young slipping out the back door and into the yard in very short time.

Mr. Young's appearance was arresting, to say the least. Tall, bony, and light-skinned, Mr. Young had riveting blue eyes, and he was fairly attractive in a spooky sort of way. One eye couldn't seem to focus, and it was partially covered with a thick white membrane called a pterygium, which was a bit frightening to look at as a kid. He always wore a brimmed hat askew, with his hair uncombed underneath. Mr. Young never cut the lawn, so the entire block from Fourth Street down to the end of Cleveland Avenue, which Bonnie's nana owned, was covered with weeds and all types of overgrowth. Wild animals – squirrels, raccoons, woodchucks – and a beehive also lived in Mr. Young's garden. It was not a place to wander into, and her nana always told her, "Baby, stay away from Mr. Young's garden." The way Nana carefully pronounced the word "garden," you knew it was a bit more than merely controlling a southern accent at play in her words.

You never knew where Mr. Young was in the garden, and he would pop out at will until the sun went down. Periodically, you could hear Mrs. Young call out shrilly from the second-story window, "Echols, you'll catch your death" or some other reference to the weather. "You better come in here!" Mr. Young would grunt a "Harrumph" and sigh before replying, "Yes, Deeear." Then he would dig around for another five minutes before turning in. Solitude had come to an end. It was time to surrender for the greater good.

It was a quietly kept secret that a neighbor who frequently took to his cups and imbibed too much liquor often got lost in Mr. Young's garden when he was really drunk. Mr. Young was so happy to have male companionship that he refused to show the man how to get out of his garden. The neighbor just had to sleep it off, come to his senses, and find his way out. Some summer evenings, you could hear the lost one howling, "Lemme outta here, man! Help me outta here!... Where's the do'... j'es lemme out!" Goodness only knows how long he was in the garden, but judging from the number of chiggers clinging to his clothing when he exited, it had to have been an extensive stay. Yes, Echols Young had the original "man cave" in the neighborhood, but all the kids were instructed to stay away from the unsightly, overgrown lot.

Mr. Young's yard was the bane of Bonnie's nana, Addie Foust's life. She hated anything unkempt and hated anyone having the ability to look in on her little acre. But she and Mr. Young were always cordial and respectful of each other's planting, sharing clippings and gardening tips. Eventually, Nana did her research and discovered that the garden was on a lot between her property and Mr. Young's that he used without the benefit of a deed. She quietly purchased the property and pushed back Mr. Young's wild garden to a more suitable distance from her little acre, her own little place of solitude and freedom from unseen, prying eyes.

Chapter 18

A DOSE OF THE GOOD LIFE

On the southeast corner of Ogle Avenue and Fourth Street lived Dr. and Mrs. Winder Porter. Unlike the homes of Bonnie's other friends, this home was a brand-new modern rancher/split-level similar to the home Bonnie's father had built for her family in Claymont. The home had a casual, elegant, blue slate front entrance with three steps to a midpoint landing and then a second set of three steps to the entrance in the opposite direction. It had beautiful red brick with white clapboards befitting the state's first Negro public health physician; his wife, Gladys, a teacher; and their two daughters, Jacquelyn, the eldest, and Marilyn, Bonnie's second ABC, or best friend in the vernacular.

The most notable thing about the Porters' residence was that Dr. Porter was in charge of this little bevy of women. Mrs. Porter had decorated the home beautifully, with the finest of furnishings carefully covered in clear plastic slipcovers for protection, which was the height of fashion and practicality in the '60s. But to the immediate right of the entrance to the living room, which was the main entry to the house, Dr. Porter positioned his huge, well-loved, lived-in recliner. From this perch, Dr. Porter oversaw his kingdom, his women and anyone who entered his domain. The recliner was in perfect alignment with his television, and if you happened to interrupt his line of sight, woe be unto you. If you were walking in the right direction, you might be asked to adjust the television aerial. On the other hand, if you were walking in the wrong direction, you might have to step lively to get out of the way quickly, if Dr. Porter's favorite show was on the air.

Dr. Porter was clearly weary at the end of the day overseeing the state's poor and the needy as well as attending to a wife and raising two daughters. It was a lot for any man. He traveled throughout the state every day, managing to administer care, keep the paperwork on his position at bay, and serve as a community leader as well. Everything in that house was directed to maintain his comfort and well-being at the end of the day. The only soft spot in his heart was for his daughters and wife. As she got to know better, Bonnie realized he attempted to maintain control with a gruff outer appearance, but he really had a heart of gold.

A man of great intelligence, Dr. Porter graduated from the University of Pennsylvania Medical College at a time when few people attended college at all, let alone earned a professional degree. He was well known for his skill and dry wit that could keep you laughing and scratching your head at the same time. His wife, a graduate of Delaware State College, taught at Stubbs Elementary School, as did Bonnie's dad.

As always, Mrs. Porter was neat as a pin. She never wore slacks and even cleaned her home dressed in starched shirtwaist dresses and lovely aprons that complemented her dresses. She was attractive and witty, and was an excellent cook, often hosting large family meals during the holidays for her extended family, which, from all of Bonnie's remembrances, was huge. Mrs. Porter maintained a careful eye over her two daughters, their friends, and their development. She made certain that the girls were well educated in the arts and the letters and well groomed, and that they were taught and displayed proper etiquette. Also, Dr. and Mrs. Porter ensured that the girls were academically challenged to the greatest extent possible. One summer, for enrichment in English and mathematics, Marilyn, Elaine White, and Bonnie attended the tony Tower Hill School, a private day school for wealthy white blue bloods, in the Delaware/Pennsylvania community referred to as "Chateau Country." During that time, Colonel Rust, the head of household for Nana's last employer, was the headmaster of the school.

The Porter girls also were known as bright, intelligent, and highly competitive athletes. It didn't matter if it was tennis, basketball, softball, swimming, or skating, Jackie and Marilyn were out in the park playing one sport or another, usually with a bunch of the guys in the neighborhood. Well-liked by all the kids in the neighborhood, the girls were recognized as scholar-athletes, which is a class unto itself. Marilyn was one of the first Negro girls to be admitted to The Girls Leader Corps at Wilmington High School, a considerable honor. Leader Corps members were recognized for their physical prowess, character, and leadership ability.

As other families in the 1960s, Dr. and Mrs. Porter lived well below their means. Everyone was thrifty because the Depression was a recent memory and white banks were reluctant to lend money to Negroes then, as now. More importantly, people were not caught up in keeping up with the Joneses. They just wanted to survive. For years, Marilyn's buddies observed Mrs. Porter shopping judiciously at Wilmington Dry Goods for her daughters' clothing when we knew the family could afford to shop at The Villager and Little Heel, where the wealthy WASPs (white Anglo-Saxon Protestants) and Jewish families whose kids attended P. S. duPont High School shopped for the latest preppy outfits for their daughters. One fine fall day, it ended, though. Marilyn showed up dressed to the nines in a gorgeous plum-colored Villager sweater, a skirt, and a bright yellow blouse complete with a circle pin on the collar. She had on Weejuns with tassels, the school shoe of the cool and well-heeled. Oh my, the times they were a changin'. Evidently, Marilyn had gotten to her dad, and a fashionista was born. She and Elaine were so notable for their trendiness they were pictured in the *Whisp*, our school newspaper, as fashion leaders. As a sophomore befriended by these two girls, Bonnie was in awe. She was part of the group – maybe on the fringe, but close enough to count. It was heaven, and life was perfect from her fifteen-year-old perspective.

About once a year, Mrs. Porter treated all of Jackie's and Marilyn's friends to an overnight at their house. All the girls would show up with pillows and blankets and stay up as late as they could, telling stories and jokes, playing table tennis, and dreaming about being "grown." They played with one another's hair, sharing styles and tips. These were the days when women set their hair in rollers and juice cans. Acne ointment was flesh-colored in a tone that suited no living human being, but was closer to the complexion of a white cadaver. Those who had dabs of this stuff on their faces looked more akin to someone dying from smallpox than being healed of a teenage pimple breakout. Beauty was something one truly suffered for and looked awful in the process of obtaining.

Often, Bonnie would hear discussions about college – Hampton University, Morgan State University, and Howard University, the historic Negro colleges and universities. Some of the girls were considering the University of California, Los Angeles and American University. The older ones spoke about the Debutante Ball, sponsored by the Alpha Kappa Alpha sorority, which introduced young ladies into Wilmington society. The girls talked and yawned until the wee hours.

Far too quickly, morning came, and Mrs. Porter gathered them together for a huge breakfast of pancakes, bacon, eggs, and hot syrup. This was really the breakfast of champions, and because they didn't know the meaning of the word *diet*, they ate heartily.

In the summer, Mrs. Porter would round them all up, and they would go "down country" to the cottage the Porters owned on the Indian River Inlet. The cottage had been passed down by the generations. The experience was like summer camp, with swimming in the lake, boat rides, and campfires. By that time, several of the older girls had licenses, and they would drive some of those in the group down in their family cars for the overnight. Mrs. Porter and her sister, whom everyone called Aunt Ted, oversaw us on these excursions. The group cooked wieners over the open fire, roasted marshmallows, and slept outside the cottage at night, lulled to sleep by the croaking of the tree frogs.

The next morning, the girls had fruit, cereal, and eggs before jumping in the river for a quick swim. Jackie would rev up the boat and take everyone for a spin around the river. It was great fun, and the trip was always over way too soon.

Time passed, and Jackie went on to attend and graduate from American University. Marilyn proceeded to high school and became one of the class leaders. She graduated from Wilmington High School and attended Cornell University and the University of Michigan School of Dentistry, where she later became the dean of students. Both girls married and had children of their own, all of whom became the scholar-athlete type that their mothers had been. Like Bonnie's wise nana said, "Apples don't fall far from the tree." It was a joy to have seen both the trees and the apples.

Chapter 19

FAVORITE HOME AWAY FROM HOME

By far, Bonnie's favorite home to visit in the neighborhood was that of James and Pearline White. They were the parents of one of Bonnie's "ace boon coons," or very best friends, in high school, Elaine Frances White. Elaine was the youngest child of four. The only female, she had three older brothers: Eugene, who was the oldest and married; Ron, a student at Yale University; and Earl, who was two years older than Elaine and, unlike most boys that age, was always kind and gentle.

In Bonnie's opinion, Elaine's parents were the most interesting people in the neighborhood. What really made them stand out was that they were obviously in love with each other – not the mushy stuff you saw on television when the story tried to convey emotion between two people, but the types of behavior that even a kid would pick up on and recognize. Bonnie's understanding was that they had been childhood sweethearts, and it showed. Whenever Bonnie came to visit, which was usually after dinner or on a Saturday, Mr. and Mrs. White would be seated at the small square table in the kitchen, perpendicular to each other, knees touching casually, leaning in toward each other, and smiling or laughing. They clearly were sharing some private bit of information. Usually, Mrs. White would throw her head back and laugh in a real infectious way that made you feel both welcome and happy. Mr. White, or "Dick," Mrs. White's nickname for her husband, would smile at her while sharing some anecdote from his day at Johnson's Pharmacy out in Hockessin, which was more of a gentleman farmer community than suburban, but decidedly white and upper middle class. To this day, the Hockessin ZIP code, 19807, is coveted by many a Delawarean.

The Whites were different in a lot of ways. Mrs. White was the only woman Bonnie knew who stayed at home and did not work, an astounding observation to Bonnie. Mrs. White was one of the most intelligent, confident women Bonnie had ever met. Her maiden name was Tildon, and the Tildons were known as people of great intelligence. Mrs. White was extremely well read and knew everything from the classics to current events. She was also knowledgeable about civil rights and African culture. Mrs. White always talked with Bonnie as though she expected her to have something meaningful to say. Most importantly, she listened to Bonnie and always left her with something to explore or research to round out her opinions, which were many and frequently needed substantiation.

Mrs. White was tall and a pretty caramel brown color. She wore her hair simply, dressed classically, and had a smile that was warm and friendly and went straight to your heart. She was encouraging and reassuring. After talking with her, you believed you could do or be anyone you wished. She was amazing and popular with young people.

Mr. White was the guiding, steady force in the White household. A bit shorter than Mrs. White, he was clearly her equal intellectually, very well read and always ready with a deep, warm laugh. He and Mrs. White seemed to share their best moments sipping tea and honey in the kitchen, Bonnie's favorite place to join them. The kitchen was always warm, and you could hear some jazz artist like Nina Simone or perhaps Miriam Makeba singing a ways off in the living room. Mr. White had beautiful snow-white hair, and he wore black horn-rimmed glasses that added to his deeply intelligent appearance. He carried himself like a serious lawyer and certainly spoke like one. Mr. White always had a good word for you and let you know he expected great things from you. He was a kind shepherd, respected by all.

Mr. and Mrs. White's great skills of encouragement and critical thinking developed three of the brightest people Bonnie had ever met. Ron entered Yale with the idea that he wanted to heal the mind, body, and soul. Bonnie had never seen or met anyone like him. He was small and wiry... kind of like a black Jiminy Cricket without a hat. He wore his hair in an uneven, textured Afro... very au courant, but in the early '60s, Ron's look was so far out in the context of sleepy Wilmington that it bordered on the weird and scary. Ron was extremely curious about everything and, when he came home to visit the house on Ogle Avenue, seemed to crackle with excitement. He brought tales of a different world and people, and he freely shared it with Bonnie. Absolutely fearless, Ron expected you to react to the world in kind. He took a particular interest in schooling Elaine and Bonnie as to how to select an undergraduate college, and he spent time educating Bonnie on the seven sister colleges and the little sisters. He also convinced Bonnie there was absolutely no other place she should consider attending school besides New England. It was, of course, the only civilized place to go in the hotbed of change occurring in this country. Ron pegged Bonnie as a Penny Pembroker, the sister school for women, a coordinated school at Brown University. "You'll have the best of all possible worlds," he said. These words led to Bonnie's matriculation at Brown University. Bonnie's mother was eternally grateful to Ron for his role in helping to point her to Brown.

Elaine's brother Earl also was considered "deep"; in other words, he was so smart they didn't know what to make of him. Also reserved, Earl was one of about three young Negro men to attend college from his high school class. A gifted writer and musician in the school band, he played basketball and hung out with the local guys, but clearly marched to a different drummer, and his parents helped to mold and shape a unique intellect and character for opportunities and a world they had only hoped to see. He matriculated at Williams College, also in Massachusetts, graduated, and proceeded to use his skills in health care.

Elaine was Bonnie's buddy. They could talk openly and frankly about almost anything. She never treated Bonnie like she was an insignificant underclassman. Elaine never thought about things the way the rest of the female teenage population did. She saw topics from a different, more nuanced angle. It didn't matter if they were discussing civil rights, boys, or teachers; Elaine examined the topic through a prism. Gently slicing away the common and the absurd, she probed the unspoken. She forced Bonnie to examine the less popular route; for example, Could resistance to unjust power be a viable alternative to nonviolent protest? Was sex before marriage really bad? Trust me, if you were even thinking like that at Wilmington High School in the '60s, you didn't mouth the words. But Elaine did.

At home, Mr. and Mrs. White and Elaine's brothers called her "Fran." When she left home for college, she dropped Elaine and became all that Fran was encouraged to be through her parents, friends, and family. Elaine was just too tight to expand into the many gifts contained in her. Fran became a student leader at Wheaton College for women in Medford, Massachusetts, encouraging diversity in the student population. She went on to earn her master's and doctorate degrees in African studies.

Later, Dr. E. Frances White became a noted author of nine books and dean of the Graduate School at New York University, fulfilling many of the goals and dreams she had discussed when she and Bonnie were youngsters wondering who, if anyone, would invite them to the school dance and if they would be accepted into the college of their choice. Fran aimed high, flew high, and never lost sight of her goal. What a role model!

Chapter 20

PLAY BALL!

She came out of Westmoreland one hot and humid summer afternoon. Peroxide-blond hair with black roots, cropped short like a boy with just enough length on the top to distinguish her as female. With a pug nose and impish blue eyes, swinging a baseball bat, she sidled up to the group of us girls at Mack Park, asking with a distinct southern twang, "Hi, I'm Dottie. Y'all wanna play some ball?" The girls were all somewhat taken aback, from the eldest in the group – Marty, Jackie, and Helen, all high school seniors – down to Bonnie, the youngest, a fifth-grader. All of them had white friends who visited their neighborhood and homes. But none of them had ever seen anyone walk down from Westmoreland into their neighborhood for any reason... or no reason. Westmoreland was an upper-class community that bordered Wilmington like a crown on the head of a ne'er-do-well relative. This community was the connector from the city to New Castle County's upper-class suburban life, better known as "Chateau Country." This portion of the county was where the duPont, Haskell, and Gates families lived. These were the estates where some of the girls' family members, such as Bonnie's nana, were employed as cooks, groundskeepers, and maids. But the most striking feature of Dottie's was that she was missing a finger. The third finger of her right hand clearly had been surgically removed, and it appeared the removal had been under duress. They were all mesmerized as they watched Dottie swing the bat casually, balancing the ridge at the end of the bat in the space where her third finger would have been.

Joyce, our city park recreational leader, home for the summer from Morgan State College, pulled them out of their reverie and quickly said, "Sure; we were just getting ready to practice. We are the Mack Park Girls Softball League. Care to join?" "Why, sure," Dottie replied with a slow, friendly grin. "I need sumpin' to do round here," she said with a grin. Bonnie couldn't believe the way Dottie spoke. She pronounced things the way her grandmother and grandfather in Claymont did. If Bonnie had even thought about speaking like that, her dad would've told her to correct her lazy tongue and speak more distinctly.

Everybody went to her assigned area of responsibility on the softball field. Marty was the pitcher, and Jackie played catcher. Helen covered first base. Marilyn was first at bat, and Dottie followed. Bonnie was somewhere in the outfield, wishing to God and the angels she could just watch from the sidelines. Never an athlete, she was struggling with the chubbies and feeling awkward. Bonnie hated sports and running and sweating. She hated being in the heat and humidity even more than that. But seeing a white girl come from Westmoreland with a missing finger was truly more interesting than anything else happening in the neighborhood that day, or any day, for that matter, and she didn't want to miss any of the action.

Marilyn was at bat, swinging sure and clean. Marty pitched the ball right over the plate, and Marilyn whacked it solidly, sending it way out over centerfield. She ran easily to second base and then stood bent with one foot on the base, rocking from one foot to the other, ready to run as soon as the next ball was hit. Fair with freckles and two red braids tossed carelessly over her shoulders, Marilyn could challenge any boy at any sport in the neighborhood – basketball, tennis, track – she did it all. She was what we called a tomboy and very happy about it. She was a smart and accomplished student, too.

Jackie sang, "Swing, batter, batter, batter, batter," punching her hand into the glove. Marty leaned back, holding the ball and glove to her chest, sizing up Dottie, who was the next batter in line. Marty glanced over her shoulder, smiled at Marilyn, and said, "Don't think

I'm not watchin' you, Marilyn." "I got her. I got her," said Marilyn's sister, Jackie. Jackie was a senior who was bold and fearless. The older of Dr. Porter's two daughters, Jackie could lift a motor off a boat and carry it into a garage thirty feet away. Boisterous and always full of fun, with a head full of bold, bright red kinky curls, Jackie kept a watchful eye over her sister and stood ready to challenge any guy who set foot in the park. A fierce competitor with a heart of mush, Jackie could always be counted on in the clutch.

Marty sent the ball across the plate toward Dottie easy and straight. No fancy stuff. No dumb stuff. Marty was a straight shooter known for her kindness and leadership. She was fun-loving with an easy grin, and was the best babysitter in the neighborhood. She clearly wanted Dottie to feel welcome, as did all of us. Unspoken though it may have been, they all wanted Dottie to feel comfortable and return so they had a complete team. Bonnie surely was not going to help them compete against the other park leagues. The Mack Park Girls Softball League needed help, a lot of it, and soon, as the season was to begin the next week. Dottie could be that help.

Dottie let the ball ease past her and had a slow, easy grin. "Girl, I know you got sumpin' more'n 'at," she said, chuckling. "C'mon wid it. Send me sumpin'!" Marty laughed as she caught the ball Jackie threw to her. "Okay," Jackie said. "She wants somethin' real. Send it to her." Jackie squatted low, bending her substantial thighs, hips hunched over her feet, one hand sending signals to Marty. Marty bent forward and nodded. She reared back and wound up in such a posture you knew something was about to be spewed out, and as a non-athlete, Bonnie was grateful she was not on the receiving end of the pitch.

Dottie leaned forward, gripping the bat with that odd three-finger grip. She swung the bat, caught a solid piece of the middle, and with a sound thwack sent the ball sailing high and deep over center field and way across the street into Mrs. Stubbs, the Realtor's yard. "Dang," Helen said. "Where in the heck did you learn to hit a ball like that?"

Marilyn took off for third base and then home. Dottie rounded the bases. When she finished, Joyce called them in to huddle around her. "That was some hit," she said. They all congratulated Dottie. "Now, how would you like to play with us this summer?" Joyce said. "You could be a big help to the team."

Dottie was a big help to the team. That summer, every evening Monday through Friday, she appeared in the park. They never knew exactly where she was living, who she was staying with, why she was there for the summer, or even her last name. But like an apparition come to life, she appeared every day, loping down the hill that curved from Westmoreland's tree-lined streets into Mack Park and the city, swinging her bat with an easy, lopsided grin, ready to play ball. There was nothing Dottie couldn't do with a bat and a ball. She could hit, run, and pitch fast, low or high. She even had a spitball that burned up the plate.

Everyone, boy and girl alike, found Dottie to be good people. Younger girls Bonnie's sister's age and her even younger buddies, Dottie Talbert and Ann Turner, all played with Dottie. She played basketball with the boys and really gave them a run for their money when her team included Marilyn, Marty, Jackie, and Helen. She was great fun, and everyone anticipated her visits during the evening. Somehow they knew it would be unkind to ask where she came from and why, or if she was staying, or where she would go to school in the fall.

Finally, they learned how she lost her third finger on her right hand. One day, they were huddled under the umbrella the city provided their Parks and Recreation leader, Joyce, for sun protection, and somebody asked Dottie how she lost the finger. "I accidentally shot it off with my rifle," she said with a cavalier air. Between the heat and the mental image of shooting a finger off with a rifle, they were all momentarily stunned into silence. "Daaaaaaaang!!!" said Helen, temporarily relieving the tension among them. Who among them owned a rifle, let alone handled it so regularly she shot herself, resulting in permanent damage? After that revelation, they all felt a bit light-headed and a little sick in the stomach. Maybe that explained why Dottie was here for the summer. Clearly, her home was in the South. They said everybody owned a gun down there, but was she there with rich white folks now or with the hired help who lived on the estate? Was her visit to help her to forget and heal, or to stop the neighbors at home from talking, or, worse yet, to prevent her from being sent to reform school or, dare one say it, jail?

The girls never voiced the questions or got any further explanation. It became part of the unspoken, unsolved mystery surrounding Dottie. It also became part of the unspoken code that they would not press any deeper into her private life. She deserved her privacy and distance just as they deserved theirs. Transitioning from childhood to womanhood was difficult enough. Having determined they didn't quite know what to say, it was clear that the best thing to do was play ball.

They played twice each week through the summer. The Mack Park Girls Softball team won all but one of its games, and those the team didn't win were close in score. Most of all, the players came to love and respect one another and the easy camaraderie they shared. The girls had become a team. They enjoyed and respected the other teams they played throughout the city at Clayton Street, Eden Park, Prices Run, and many others. Every team was struck by Dottie. Mack Park was the only integrated team in the city, and her three-fingered hand was a knockout. It struck fear and awe in the girls' opponents and gave them a one-upmanship, an odd and unique competitive edge.

The summer heat began to cool, and one evening, when the first cool, crisp air of fall was recognizable, Dottie didn't show up at the park to play ball. She never came down the curved, tree-lined streets of Westmoreland again that summer or the next. The girls often wondered and talked about where Dottie had gone and why she never said good-bye. But she left as she came, unexpectedly and without fanfare. Maybe she was an apparition clothed in flesh or a spunky angel on assignment portending things to come. Who knows? One thing's for sure, though: She sure was a great ballplayer.

Chapter 21

TOUCHED BY GOD

S t. Matthew's Episcopal Church was the crossroads of the hired help of the white landed gentry of the community and the educated and upwardly mobile Negro community in Wilmington produced by the educational opportunities created by the GI Bill at the close of World War II. The hired help – the Negro butlers, maids, cooks, and laundresses – at the encouragement of their employers began to attend services for the coloreds originally held at St. Andrew's Episcopal Church in downtown Wilmington. The Episcopal Church had a history of being sympathetic to matters of injustice, and the Negro surely had been treated unjustly in Delaware and, specifically, Wilmington. It was a natural extension of this philosophy of injustice that there should be a focus on addressing the needs of Negroes, including their spiritual needs, in Wilmington. Bonnie's nana, Addie Brown Foust, began attending St. Andrew's not long after she began working in Wilmington. Over time, the number of attendees at the church grew in sufficient number, such that it was clear that there should be a parish established for Negroes interested in serving God in the thoughtful, intellectual, quiet, reflective manner of the Episcopal Church.

So in 1950, St. Matthew's Episcopal Church was built on the corner of 7th and Walnut Streets, on the edge of the East Side of Wilmington, within walking distance and the shadow of St. Andrew's Episcopal Church. Bonnie's nana became a founding member and began a long relationship with the church as a faithful tither. Never one to seek position or power, Nana's objective was to get right and be right with the Lord. St. Matthew's was a far cry from the tent meetings and hay bales of North Carolina, but certain principles of faith in God remained the same no matter whose pew one sat in. Tithing, daily Bible study, and prayer were her foundations, and she passed them along to her child and her grandchildren. Because they adored Nana, they each have done their best to follow and honor her example, and to teach her great-grandchildren these principles of faith.

St. Matthew's had a simple red brick exterior facade with only one stained-glass window, behind the altar on the second floor, not easily seen from the street. The entry at ground level was plain red double doors that admitted you to a granite-lined entrance. You could take the broad, gray stone steps up to the sanctuary or enter into a single door on the left that led to the undercroft – which housed the pastor's office, the choir room, and the restrooms – or you could step down into an area that served multiple purposes: as the cafeteria, auditorium, and classroom. This simple building layout also tended to direct you to the part of the building that could best address your concerns. If it was God you needed, then you'd proceed to the second floor. If it was a man-related, more earthbound issue you wished to resolve, then you'd step to the left.

From a child's perspective, the building was filled with wonder on the second floor. The Episcopal service was filled with every element that would make one believe he or she was in heaven or sitting close to God during the service. You knew you weren't in heaven, but surely you had left earth for another plane. It had great pageantry, wonderfully colored cassocks, and robes with braids and tassels. It also had candles and crosses hoisted high above one's head, and there was the elixir of the incense... a sweet, pungent odor of frankincense and myrrh that Beily said floated their prayers to Jesus.

Every service began with a procession headed by the priest, dressed in a beautiful embroidered robe, the lettering in Latin, the sash and tails festooned with brightly colored tassels. Father Wilson, who was Trinidadian, sang and chanted with a soft Caribbean lilt to his voice that lifted you high into the heavens and the presence of the Lord. The acolytes followed Father Wilson. They were handsome young men, carefully groomed, dressed in beautiful crisp black or red cassocks with starched white surplices. Their hair, styled in a precision cut known as a quo vadis, was carefully brushed from kinks to waves smooth enough to make you seasick. Like beautiful young Greek gods, their strong, sinewy arms lifted the candelabras and the cross above our heads as they walked down the center aisle. As they approached each row, everyone bowed his or her head in submission and obedience to Christ, the risen King, Son of our Father, God.

The choir, comprised of the gifted, the willing, and the wannabes, followed the acolytes. The choir was mostly female of every shape and size, along with three or four men with bass and baritone voices, of strong enough character to resist the moldy and oldy females in need of reassurance of their feminine wiles. Two members were outstanding, though, because of the way they walked down the center aisle. All women wore high heels at this time, but Ms. Nancy Hill and her sister, Sharon, rocked the Atlantic and Pacific Oceans when they gracefully turned, swept the congregation with their round, wide, thickly lashed eyes, and carefully glided down the aisle, swaying gently from side to side. Ever so tastefully, like two gazelles, they ascended the stairs to the altar and quickly reached their seats in the choir loft. Oh, how many eyes slyly cut sideways instead of looking straight ahead at the altar and how many sighs slipped silently from the lips of old men watching those sisters bring the choir in with their magic.

The organist, Venti Williams, controlled the service. She was classically trained and played the organ beautifully. In fact, Mrs. Williams gave piano lessons, and Bonnie and her sister, Beily, were both students in her Saturday program. Mrs. Williams knew all the high-toned classical music required for the anthems, interludes, and intricate musical format of the service.

However, it seemed that Mrs. Williams was waging a not-so-quiet, undeclared war against the members of the congregation, the choir, and against Father Wilson, too. Her weapon of choice: her organ. She played so loudly as to drown out the choir and Father Wilson, and at times she even managed to challenge the acolytes. As the music director at the church, Mrs. Williams wielded a heavy mallet. Through her control over the volume of the organ, she seemed to be saying: "You numskulls wouldn't even have a service without me. You need to recognize that and pay homage to me right now. But in case you've forgotten, take that!!" And Venti would pull out the stops and up the volume of the organ until the very rafters shook. Babies in the audience would cry, and little children would put their fingers in their ears. Choir members would roll their eyes to the heavens, seeking relief from God Himself. Father Wilson would chant, "Good Lord, deliver us." The congregation would strain to sing over Mrs. Williams' volume, but she would just snap those stops open even more, and the volume would increase to deafening levels. Mrs. Williams would close her eyes and rock back and forth on her organ bench as though she were caught up in the rapture, completely oblivious to the presence of any other living beings, as the organ's volume increased and increased until she hit a high-pitched E-flat chord. She held the chord for what seemed like an indeterminable period, her back stiff, frozen in position, she and her organ.

Finally, with a self-satisfied grin and a chuckle, she would relent. Slowly, she became conscious of the existence of others. Her rocking slowed. She turned the volume of the organ to a whisper, gently pushing the stops back in place close to the backboard of the organ, eventually returning the organ to the rest position. Gently slumping back into her seat, her hands relaxed, flaccid in her lap, Venti quietly contemplated her next attack. The choir and the congregation, Venti's victims, gasped for breath and fell into their seats exhausted and nearly asphyxiated from the struggle with the organist.

Now came the acolytes, the young, gifted, male, tall and reed slender, dressed to dazzle the young girls and encourage the hearts of the old that yes, Lord, we are making progress, we shall overcome. These young men moved with the precision of a trained military team. They moved in unison, genuflecting before the altar in precise uniformity, lighting the candles at exactly the same moment, striking the domed bell that called the congregation to repentance before Holy Communion was served. These men took a white ritual and transformed it into a distinctly black thing without denigrating the Lord or the Episcopal tradition. It was a harbinger of things to come from the younger generations of Negroes, soon to be blacks, in Wilmington. They put their unique imprimatur on a formerly staid, lifeless everyday activity of worship and made it their own while demonstrating their racial pride through the process. They took great pride in their service to the Lord, and it made all our hearts – those of parents, young girls, Father Wilson, and congregants – swell with pride. The Bible says, "Ye shall know them by their fruits" (Matthew 7:16). The fruit of St. Matthew's was good!

St. Matthew's was a special place for its congregants and the community. It hosted dances for the young as part of the Episcopal Young Churchmen. It sponsored the Playcrafters as an artistic venue for its young adults. It provided leadership development for service on other community boards through participation in the Vestry. It provided basic training in the understanding of the Bible through the Sunday school program for youths.

One of the most celebrated activities in the church was confirmation Sunday. For the participating youths, it was the formal demarcation between childhood and adulthood. Once you had mastered the catechism and had been confirmed by the bishop, you were invited to partake in all the rights and responsibilities as an adult in the Episcopal Church. You could participate in Communion, tithe, join the adult choir, and more.

119

Confirmation was an important ceremony. The bishop came down to St. Matthew's from St. John's Cathedral. All the girls wore white dresses they had shopped for with their mothers for the event, and the church provided white veils. Because Bonnie was in the throes of the chubbies, her mother took her to DiMaura's, a special dress store in the Little Italy section of Wilmington on Fourth and Lincoln Streets. This was the only store in town that sold special event dresses for little girls. They spent several hours going through dresses before they found the perfect one for her. It was absolutely lovely, white with a princess-cut bodice, creating curves in a thick middle; an embroidered overskirt, sculpting hips gently; and a wide sash that nicely defined her waist. Thank God for Beily's taste and patience. Bonnie looked almost slim and, most importantly, she looked like a bride for Christ. For many of them, it was the first time they were allowed to wear heels. In Bonnie's case, she was allowed to wear spoolies, which were heels about the height and width of a spool of thread. They provided just enough lift to acknowledge that you were in transition from childhood to womanhood, but also enough distinction that you knew you were not grown yet. No grown woman was ever spotted in a pair of spoolies; in fact, you couldn't find them sold outside the preteen shoe section of any store.

Confirmation Sunday was a big event in the church. Everything was spit-spot clean. The floors were waxed and shimmering like mirrors, the faint smell of incense was in the air, and, most notably, a huge chair was positioned just below the altar and obviously awaiting THE BISHOP! Those of us who were going to be confirmed were lined up downstairs, listening to the crowd gathering above. Our parents walked us downstairs to the undercroft, where we awaited instructions from the priest, Father Casson. Bonnie's catechism class was fairly large, and it was comprised of Sunday school class members she'd attended church with for many years. It was a coming-of-age ceremony for them, and their parents, family, friends, and congregants all looked forward to the event. Nana had managed to get the day off, and Beily was dressed in a particularly fetching suit from Fischer's. Boo and Skip were there wishing they were home playing with their buddies, but in this day and time, you went where Momma went, and you asked no questions.

As those who were to be confirmed, we were most interested in the coffee hour that would be at the end of the ceremony, during which treats and goodies would be available for those being confirmed and their guests. Among the class were Emile Gardner, every preteen girls' heartthrob; Hilmar Jensen, who was sweet and funny, cute as a button, and smart as a whip; Cassandra Lee and her brother George, silent, stoic, and ever watchful; and Rosalind Lewis, bright, quiet with a low voice that sounded like she'd swallowed Drano, and with the most beautiful coffee-and-cream complexion Bonnie had ever seen. Our faithful Sunday schoolteacher, Mr. O'Neal, was present. He was always kind and patient with us during class. We were a fairly rambunctious group, but he managed us with a firm and loving touch. Mrs. Marshall, Thurgood's sister, was there, and dear Mrs. Gant, a white woman who was a member of St. Andrew's congregation and who took a particular interest in "the Negro." She had been an active participant in our Christian development, exposing us to missions in Africa and Jewish seders. You never realize what a gift adults like this are until you are the adult attempting to provide services to the next generation as these sages once served you.

They lined up for the confirmation service, and Mrs. Williams began to play the organ. The bishop arrived, and the procession was organized, with the catechism class bringing up the rear. The first three rows on the right were reserved for them. The class walked down the aisle to the designated point of entry. An acolyte was posted at the pew so there would be no mistakes. We stood until signaled by the priest, Father Casson, that it was time to be seated. Each of us fidgeted in our seats, trying so hard to look serious and grown up, but our physical unrest belied our state of mind. We were still kids, and today we were pretending to be grown up.

The service began. A series of chants and responses between the bishop and the priest stated that St. Matthew's had several young people to be presented by St. Matthew's to the bishop for confirmation. Suddenly, it was time to present the class. We stood up, and one by one, our names were called. We kneeled before the bishop, and he laid hands on us. We had been touched by God! We had been transformed. Finally, we could drink the magical wine that made us part of Jesus, the Lamb of God! But really we just wanted to drink the wine. It was the wine that made the ceremony such a big deal to us kids. Our relationship with Christ didn't really solidify until much later, but our parents had done their best to give us one foot into heaven. We were each presented a copy of the Episcopal *Book of Common Prayer* and a certificate of our confirmation that day. It culminated with kisses from our family, pats on our heads by other adult congregants, and comments like, "You've grown to be such a lovely young lady. I know your mother is proud." It was an all-around feel-good day for all.

Time moved on, and as a parish, St. Matthew's did not have the income to select and support its own priest, but was dependent upon an itinerant circuit and the bishop to select who should be at the head of St. Matthew's. Father Wilson moved on, and he was followed by a well-loved former acolyte, Father Lloyd Casson. Father Casson was a gifted leader, much too big to stay in Wilmington with St. Matthew's. He loved us, nurtured us, and forced us to push forward and grow. Lloyd clearly had a rocket in his pocket. His abilities were noted, and all too quickly, he was promoted to the National Cathedral in Washington, D.C. Several other people were appointed to serve at St. Matthew's, none of whom captured the hearts of the people or the community, and certainly none who eclipsed his love and service. All the others were carpetbaggers just marking time until they could move on to their "real assignment," where they could really shine. In the meantime, they took advantage of the vacuum Father Lloyd and Father Wilson had left behind and filled the space on their resume or made a few shekels before retiring. Wilmington and its people were never worthy of their love or admiration. St. Matthew's was just a check mark to say they'd done the job, and off they went, smelling themselves and their supposed superiority.

This type of leadership continued for decades, until one day, God smiled and Father Casson, now Canon Casson, came home to breathe the breath of life over God's scorched and dead people. Like the parable of the dry bones, he led them back to life. He offered them love, structure with relationship, a reigniting of their faith, and relationship with God. He reunited St. Andrew's and St. Matthew's, forming the hip new SAM's place, and got them moving in Christ again. Canon Lloyd Casson refused to allow the historic black Episcopalian Church to die in Wilmington, and for that many owe him a debt of honor and thanks. His legacy will live on for many decades.

Chapter 22

SAVE THE LAST DANCE FOR ME

One Saturday night in November 1965, the gym at Wilmington High School was dimmed. Motown was blaring over the loudspeakers, and clumps of students of all races and creeds from fifteen to eighteen years old were gathered around the periphery of the gym. Three girls were positioned at the right of the entrance: Marilyn Porter, Elaine "Fran" White, and Bonita "Bonnie" Byrd. The three were fast buddies. Bookish and accomplished students, but hip in their own way, the three were young intellectuals looking for opportunities to be cool. Dressed in their Saturday night best, they observed the incoming crowd, waving at friends who entered the gym, practicing their latest cha-cha, and swaying to the beat. Marilyn and Fran were sophisticated juniors. Bonnie was a newly entered sophomore, but she'd already distinguished herself as a first honor roll member, a cheerleader, and a class officer.

She'd been invited to the dance by a nice boy, Vic, a senior on the basketball team, and she had every intention of going to the prom with him. As she and her buddies watched the entryway, four good-looking guys, not students of Wilmington High, approached the doorway. She recognized one of them from church: Ed "Lucky" Stone. He had beautiful curly lashes and was smart, but too tall and a bit challenging. Bonnie dismissed him quickly from the list of possibilities.

"Who is that?" she whispered to her friend Marilyn, who had waved to a cute guy who had caught her attention. "That's Butch Williams, honey," she replied. "Out of your league, All City Student Council." "Well, just watch my smoke," Bonnie snorted as she smoothed her white piqué collar and tugged at the skirt of her black empire dress with the watch plaid bodice. She looked down at her black Pappagallo flats. *What guy in his right mind could resist me?* she thought as she patted her bob carefully in place, coaxing a curl into position on her cheek. "Introduce me," Bonnie said. "Okay," Marilyn said as she stepped toward him. "Hi, Butch," she said. "Hey, Marilyn," he replied. "This is my friend, Bonnie Byrd," she said. Bonnie could feel herself melting as he grinned his megawatt smile toward her. *Be calm, girl*, she thought. *Ooh, he's sooo cute... and those eyes.* Nobody like that was at Wilmington High School. Nobody. "Hey, nice to meet you!" he replied evenly and easily, gazing directly into her eyes. *Lord, I hope he doesn't think I'm too fat*, she thought. "Didn't I see you cheering for the wrong team?" he said with a grin. "Yeah, I cheer for high school," Bonnie said, matching his smile with her own. She lifted her chin and glanced down demurely. *I hope he can't see my heart pumping*, she thought. The thumping was so loud in her ears she just knew he could hear it too.

"Save the last dance for me," he said smoothly as he and his buddies walked away.

"Butch Williams," she heard another cheerleader, Wanda Ward, squeal as he walked away. Wanda was as cute as they came with a pixie haircut and a squeaky voice. She was popular, fun, and smart. Her subject of choice: mathematics. Currently, she was going with a football player in her class, Madric, who also seemed to be familiar with Butch. *Popular guy*, Bonnie thought. Well, here was Vic. Time to dance. She'd think about Butch later, as her eyes would periodically search the room for him.

Butch moved easily throughout the room, stopping to chat here and there. He was there from the rival team, Pierre S. duPont High School, making a show of goodwill. The time passed quickly and pleasantly.

Before anyone knew it, the last dance was being called. Vic had gone to retrieve Bonnie's coat before the cloakroom got too crowded. Bonnie stood close to the exit, just within the shadows. Marilyn and Fran had left with their respective dates, Ray and Turtle, both football players. Frankly, Bonnie was disappointed. Butch had promised her the last dance. She looked down at her toes... the feet of a princess... Nana had always said she had the feet of a princess... small with no calluses. *Oh, well, the princess won't get the prince tonight*, she thought as she sighed.

Two suede bucks approached her range of vision. "Last dance," she heard the low, husky request. She looked up to see two round, mischievously twinkling hazel eyes smiling into her eyes. His hand was extended slightly toward her.

"Sure," she replied, her even tone belying a heart skipping wildly, unevenly. Butch pulled her gently toward him. He wrapped his arms around her and put his cheek just at the top of her head. She could hardly breathe she was so excited and happy. *Lord, I hope he doesn't get any Ultra Sheen on his chin,* she thought. He smelled so good and clean, and the crisp starch on his high-boy collar told her this boy was dressed to impress. Heaven could have gone on forever, but she opened her eyes to find Vic standing at the edge of the gym, waiting with her coat.

"Thanks for the dance," Butch said as he pulled away. "G'night," Bonnie answered weakly, her weakness due as much to the last dance as how she would explain the situation to Vic.

Chapter 23

AN EXPERIENCE OF A LIFETIME

After some fits and starts, Butch Williams and Bonnie became an item. He passed the ultimate test, though, when he happened to come by one evening when Nana was home. Nana had just baked cookies, and Bonnie invited him to come in and have some goodies. After formal introductions, Butch settled down and in a charming manner spoke with Nana about his family and his aspirations. She observed him carefully and listened intently, smiling pleasantly. Shortly thereafter, he left, heading for a basketball pickup game at the park not far from their home. Bonnie walked him to the door and wished him a good game.

Nana stood in the dining room and said, "He's a nice young man. Very polite. You have my permission to continue seeing him." "Thank you, Nana," Bonnie said. She'd brought one other date home... though you couldn't even equate him to a date. He was just a guy walking Bonnie home, but Nana had let her know, "That is not it!" Nothing else was said. Nothing else needed to be. Bonnie never let the boy walk her home again. In fact, she never saw him again except to say hi in passing in the hallway at school.

But Butch got the approval sign, so Nana obviously saw something in him that warranted approval – something beyond Bonnie's "Oh, he's sooo cute" gushing that merited Nana's stamp of recognition. She had been quietly schooling Bonnie on what a woman should look for in a husband, offering such comments as, "When a woman looks for a husband, she needs to think about her children." Initially, Bonnie thought Nana meant the guy should be cute, but as Bonnie got older, she understood it was a lot deeper than that. Could he provide for children? What type of role model would he be for children? Did he even want to have children? Could we agree on how to raise children?

Nana often used the people she worked for to teach lessons. For example, there was a difference between having money or an education and being well bred. One of her employers had given birth to a child sired by a stable hand in her youth. The child had grown into an overweight, rather slovenly adult who smoked often and had skin of a poor, swarthy quality. The second child of this woman was sired by a person of means and standing, "old money," and good bloodlines reaching back centuries. The offspring of this marriage was tall, slender, and blond. She cut quite a different figure around the pool. From Nana's perspective, the truth was obvious. Marry on par with your class at the very least, never down. There were some things transmitted by genes that money, education, position, and power simply could not overcome.

It meant a lot to Bonnie that Nana liked Butch. He had passed the Beily and the Nana tests. Only one to go, Dad, and that might be a bit touchy. Dad didn't seem to like any boys, except her brother, and he was blood. Bonnie would need to wait to arrange some things... right timing and setting meant everything when dealing with Dad.

No doubt, Butch and Bonnie were developing a friendship and relationship that was meaningful. They'd discussed current events, the war, women's issues, sex, and civil rights. Bonnie tended to be quite conservative with most things, and he pushed more to the left. They'd argue their positions pretty ferociously. Sometimes Bonnie didn't expect him to ever call again, but he did. He called so much that her sister and brother constantly complained about Bonnie hogging the phone, and Beily would tell her she'd have to get off for a while and let them use it.

Going to college, preparing the application, and how to pay for college were major topics of discussion for them. Butch was a gifted scholar-athlete; he had been selected as one of fifty young men to participate in the Upward Bound Program at the University of Delaware in the summer of 1966. Part of the Trio Programs begun as part of President Johnson's War on Poverty, Upward Bound was designed to provide academic enrichment for students with the potential to matriculate at an accredited university. Upward Bound, aka UBP, also sought to familiarize the participants with the rigors of study and life on a university campus. Benefits also accrued to the sponsoring university. The program provided the participating university the opportunity to get a firsthand look at local academic talents before other competing universities, it gave them standing in the community as contributing to the War on Poverty, and those coveted federal dollars eased any pain they may have experienced in the process of opening their doors to underprivileged African-American children.

The director of the Upward Bound Program at the University of Delaware was Richard "Dickey" Wilson, a former teacher in Wilmington Public Schools. Mr. Wilson was like a pied piper of sorts, traveling the length and breadth of the "Diamond State" seeking talented African-American students who would challenge long-held racist perceptions of an established white university through their academic performance and conduct. Phase one of the program implementation at the U of D was to begin with fifty young men. Phase two involved the recruitment of fifty young men and fifty young women a grade level below the current class. Mr. Wilson plumbed the talent of his existing students. Because Bonnie was Butch's girl, he gave Mr. Wilson a heads-up about her. Along with one other girl at her high school, Bonnie was recruited to participate in the first group of females in the Upward Bound Program at the University of Delaware. It was the experience of a lifetime and one that impacted Bonnie's life for years to come.

Upward Bound provided an away-from-home experience for eight weeks during the summer before students' eleventh and twelfth grades in high school. It provided arts and cultural experiences and a weekly twenty-five-dollar stipend for the student so that spending change did not become a barrier to student participation. Participants had a full course load of mathematics, science, and English five days a week from 8:30 AM till 2 PM, including composition and research assignments in the main library on campus. At the close of the summer, each student had the opportunity to work so they could earn some money before returning to school. Upon graduation, participating students were assigned to work at a major corporation that supported the program. In Delaware, this included E. I. duPont de Nemours, Hercules, ICI, NVF, and many more.

Learning to live communally was an important aspect of life at UBP. Everyone except the counselors shared a room with someone. On Bonnie's first day at the program, her mother brought her to the university and signed her into the Rodney dormitory. Her roommate hadn't arrived, so she busied herself putting things away, making up her bed, and peaking out of the room periodically to see who else might have moved in down the hall or next door. Soon she heard a sound at the door and turned to see a pretty girl with shoulder-length hair, beige skin, and kind eyes enter the room. Her diminutive mother was behind her. "Hi!" they said at the same time. The girl giggled pleasantly. "I'm Lillian. Lillian LaFate." "I'm Bonnie Byrd," Bonnie replied. "I guess this makes us roommates." They giggled as she and her mom put away what appeared to be a zillion new dresses, all from LeRoy's Style Shop, an upscale dress shop in town.

Lillian and Bonnie quickly became friends. She was clear about her career aspirations; she wanted to become a nurse. It was how she saw herself. Everything she thought about in terms of studies had to do with nursing. Bonnie knew her mother and Lillian's mom would like each other and get along well, so Bonnie couldn't wait to introduce them. They shared their family stories, about brothers... She was the oldest of seven, they all had French names, and Lillian was the only girl – no sisters. Both of them had divorced parents. Both of them had plans to be somebody someday. They were definitely going to college; though they weren't sure of the particulars, they knew it was going to happen.

Lil, as Bonnie came to call her, and she had fun. They were a perfect match. They would eat together most times, do hair together, and sometimes even study together. Lillian had a beautiful deep contralto voice and often sang hymns in the shower or when she was just fooling around. She was deeply religious and had strict rules about no pants and not shaving that Bonnie didn't understand, but it seemed to work for Lil. She always had male attention. One guy in particular, whom she nicknamed "Panther" because he was a beautiful mahogany brown and slick, was her special boyfriend. Panther constantly called Lil over the intercom in the morning so he could walk her to class. He would call, hold down the speaker button, and call, "Lil-LEEEEE-unnnnnn, Lil-LEEEEE-unnnnnn," in a semi-melodic way. Lillian did not budge from the bed. Bonnie could take it during the week, but on Saturdays, when there was no urgency to rise and shine, it would make her nuts!

Classes at UBP were wonderful. The teachers were excellent and challenged them to go beyond their best. They stretched the students' understanding of the world through studies, and Bonnie thoroughly enjoyed every minute of it. It was exciting to be in class with students from across the state who enjoyed academics. Every week ended in a battery of tests, but they were all prepared. Somehow the participants knew the program was important and that it played a part in the Civil Rights movement that was so ever present on television. They knew the results of their performance would be sent to Washington and that the future of other students and their opportunities rested squarely on their backs. It was a bit daunting, but it was de rigueur for the day. African-American youths had inherited the struggle to move their race forward. They had to do what their parents could not. It was just the way it was.

Saturdays were the best day at UBP. First of all, you would visit Mr. Wilson at his office to pick up your stipend. Twenty-five dollars was a lot of money in 1966. You could buy an outfit at the General Store on Main Street, get an ice cream sundae, and still have enough money for your laundry, toiletries, and necessities. You were responsible for budgeting your funds and handling your own business. The rest of Saturday was usually spent getting ready for a cultural event. Sometimes they would take a trip to Washington or New York for the whole day. On other occasions, they might go to the Uptown Theater for the Motown Review. Whatever they did, everyone spent the day getting ready for the evening out. Girls washed and rolled hair. Guys starched and ironed their shirts and pants. On the way out of the dorm for an evening of fun, Butch would ask Bonnie, "How do I look? Am I dressed for success?" Her reply was, "You're so sharp you're wounded." When they left the university, they did honor to Mr. Wilson, the university, and their parents. They were proud and honored to participate in UBP, and you didn't need to look hard to figure it out.

Their UBP group formed a close-knit group of friends and competitors. As they grew, they challenged one another to do their best, supported one another as colleagues, moved out into the greater society with a confidence born of experience and nurturing that Dickey Wilson built for them, brick by brick, at great sacrifice to himself and his family. His desire for their success exceeded his desire to protect himself physically and politically. He allowed them to love him, and he became everything to them.

Later, many of the UBP students matriculated at the university; others, at Delaware State College (now University) or another college or university. It all began with Dickey's vision for their futures and America's. The Upward Bound Programs performed so well nationwide that they were gutted of their original purpose and content, and now serve as mere shadows of their former selves. It reminds this nation that we know what we need to do to maximize the talents of our citizenry when we want to or think we need to. How long will it take to rekindle the spirit? It's anyone's guess. The author prays that it is soon, though, before those old enough to remember have expired and the collective memory is no longer archived for research.

Chapter 24

THE KING IS DEAD

High school was moving at a fast clip. Bonnie was a senior, and a lot had happened. Fortunately, she had earned a National Achievement Scholarship from the National Merit Scholarship Program. Bonnie was home alone the Saturday morning the letter from National Merit Corporation arrived acknowledging her award of the scholarship. She opened the letter, somewhat incredulous at the contents. She turned to the mirror and looked at herself in amazement. Bonnie turned her face to the heavens and said: "Thank You, God. I know this gift is from You. Thanks a lot. I really needed it." The only other student in the state who had been awarded this scholarship was her neighbor, Ernest Talbert Jr., the smartest person in the whole of Wilmington High School. Ernie was the only person Bonnie had ever met who could take physics, chemistry, and calculus, never study, and get A's. He earned a 1600 on his SATs and never cracked a practice book. That was what Bonnie called smart. In comparison, Bonnie was just a good plugger.

The scholarship was important to Bonnie, though. It afforded her four thousand dollars a year to attend any accredited college or university of her choice. She knew she could attend college now without putting a strain on her momma's household budget.

Skipper was growing by leaps and bounds, eating everything that wasn't nailed down. The fifteen dollars a week in child support that her dad paid for Bonnie helped a little bit, but she knew when things got tight because Beily would find a job catering, or a summer job training certified nursing assistants or working the night shift at the

Veterans Administration. She didn't want to add to the financial strain on her, so it was important to select a school within the budget and one where she could get work to support herself.

Bonnie's guidance counselor, Madeline Bauer, had done everything she could to discourage her from applying to college. "You may think you're a good student around here," she'd say. "You'll be lucky if Delaware State accepts you." Beily was so angry she took the afternoon off from work to speak to Mr. Martin, the principal, and Ms. Bauer. She informed Ms. Bauer that she was carefully cultivating her children, their goals for life beyond high school, and their college choices. She did not appreciate Ms. Bauer's interference, and she would appreciate Mr. Martin's support. Needless to say, Ms. Bauer did little to interfere with Bonnie's trajectory thereafter.

Bonnie's initial choice for college was Jackson College for Women at Tufts University in Medford, Massachusetts. The tuition expenses at the school exceeded the scholarship financial package she had, so Bonnie ended up selecting Brown University of Providence, Rhode Island. She had applied there because of Ron White's pronouncement years ago that she was a Penny Pembroker. The curriculum for the different colleges was challenging, and the pictures of the campus seemed nice enough. There were no pictures of African-Americans, but the University of Delaware didn't have any pictures in its catalog, although she knew students there, notably Butch Williams. She couldn't afford a trip to the campus, but its reputation was solid, and Beily was pleased. So Brown it was.

Spring was just starting to peek its head out, and it was the kind of sweet, slightly warm day when you decided to wear a jacket, not a coat, just because you were sick of the winter weather. The crocuses and forsythias were starting to bud, and Bonnie was looking forward to Easter break, which was right around the corner.

All her close buddies had graduated from high school the

previous year. Linda, Barbara, and Sharon all had boyfriends, so their time was taken. Dating was the bright line in racial relations, even among friends. Butch was at the University of Delaware studying mathematics and biology in preparation for a career as an optometrist, and life just wasn't as much fun as it had been. Bonnie spent a lot of time visiting Mrs. White after school, and Lillian and she hung out on Saturdays sometimes, but by and large senior year was not joyous.

Lil was great fun, though. Her dad worked at Chrysler and always kept a long Chrysler Imperial. One Saturday, Mr. LaFate let Lil take the car for a spin. It was a beautiful ragtop, and of course, they drove it with the top down so all of Wilmington could see them in their glory. They'd each bought a pair of inexpensive Jackie O look alike sunglasses in the Five and Dime Store that they placed on their faces at a rakish angle. They drove up and down Market Street, eyeing cute guys with a, "Hey baby" and a wink. If the guys responded, the girls sped off, too scared to stay and talk. They just sped away, giggling like two silly teenagers, carefree and unaware of how short this happy, carefree period in their lives really was.

On Thursday, April 4, 1968, toward the close of the day, Bonnie was walking down the hallway toward her math class when suddenly, she could hear screams, crashes, and glass breaking. *What in the world could be going on?* Bonnie thought. "They killed him! They killed him!" she heard. A group of kids ran flying past Bonnie. One boy stopped and smashed a window. Another group of kids went running through the building screaming, kicking the lockers. Bonnie didn't recognize any of the boys running by, which she thought was odd. But who was killed, and why were they acting like this?

Ernie Talbert was at the door to class. "You better come in here," he said as he opened the door. "What's going on?" "I think they shot Dr. King," he said in a quiet, even tone. "What!" Bonnie replied almost incredulous that something like this could happen. The screaming and noise outside their classroom continued. Suddenly, they were interrupted by an announcement on the intercom. "Ladies and gentlemen, it has been reported that Dr. Martin Luther King Jr. was shot in Memphis, Tennessee, earlier today. Vandals have been roaming the hallways, but the building is now secure. Please get your belongings and exit the building immediately. School reopening will be announced on your local radio stations."

They all exited the classroom soberly, appearing somewhat confused and dismayed. Most of them had the books they needed to study and just proceeded to walk home.

As Bonnie walked toward 301, she could see several spirals of smoke in the distance and hear the rat-a-tat-tat of gunfire in the distance. Could Wilmington be having a riot? Not here, she thought. *Things weren't perfect, by a long shot, but had frustration reached a point where we're shooting at one another and setting fire to buildings?*

Later that evening, their worst fears were realized. Mayor Babiarz had contacted Governor Charles Terry and requested that the state police be sent into Wilmington to control the populace, stop the looting and burning, and restore order to the city. The West Side of Wilmington along the "valley," where many of Bonnie's classmates resided, was on fire. Governor Terry, overreacting by all accounts, decided to send in the National Guard instead of the state police. By five that evening, they could hear the roll and bump of armed jeeps patrolling the perimeter of their little community on the hill.

The heart of the riot seemed to have focused on West Center City, one of the most densely populated portions of the city. Little Italy, close to Bonnie's home, was said to be in arms, and it was rumored that no one black should even try to drive in the area, even though plenty of blacks lived on duPont and Lincoln Streets in Little Italy. Browntown and Hedgeville, on the southwest part of Center City, home of the Polish and Lithuanian populations, also were armed and extremely dangerous. A good fourth of Bonnie's classmates lived here. Bonnie had shared chrusciki for years among these families, worked on Student Council elections in the different classmates' homes, and attended the Girls Club in this neighborhood. *What was Wilmington coming to?* she thought. *What could we, as youths, do to help heal the situation?*

Several of her classmates got on the telephone to discuss the matter, and they decided they needed a peace march. It would start at Wilmington High and proceed right down the center of Fourth Street in the center of the riots. Robert Evans, a classmate of Bonnie's from fifth grade; Joe Green; and several other guys spread the word among their black classmates. Pete Luce, whose father was a Presbyterian minister working in Center City, negotiated on behalf of Center City residents, and Ernie Talbert gathered the rest of their class. The march was a huge success and well received.

Unfortunately, the riots continued, and by the end of the week, Governor Terry had sent in more than thirty-five hundred troops to station behind Pierre S. duPont High School in the northeast section of the city. Wilmington remained occupied until Russell Peterson was elected governor and Hal Haskell was elected mayor of Wilmington in November 1971.

Nothing changed until these two men took office in January 1972, despite the pleadings of the corporate community and the National Democrat Party leadership. Cholly still had a choke hold on the lovely little "Diamond State"; oddly, it took the Republican Party to break its hold on the City of Wilmington. One should pause and think about this lesson. One should reflect on the outcome of this historic message. What lessons does it offer one to consider in the context of today's racial struggles?

Chapter 25

A PICTURE OF CREATIVITY

Our little community on the hill had the usual mix of teachers, doctors, lawyers, and professionals. It had good, solid postal and factory workers. However, by far, the most unique community members were those who made their living through the arts and entertainment fields. About two blocks west of Bonnie's home, on the corner of Ogle and Conrad Streets, was the home of Mr. and Mrs. Edward Loper. Mr. Loper was a well-known painter in the state. He painted in the cubist style that Picasso had popularized in the 1950s and '60s. Mr. Loper gave art lessons, and, most intriguing to the neighborhood children, he often posed his wife nude or seminude in the backyard for works of art he was creating. Bonnie's mom carefully explained to them the beauty of the human body and why it was a good subject for art, but for a group of prepubescent and adolescent girls doubtful and anxious about the daily changes they discovered in their own bodies, it was just too weird and uncomfortable.

But then again, everything about the Lopers was different. They were an integrated couple. He was a tall, rather imposing, dignified black man. He often wore a black beret, and he had a goatee. He reminded Bonnie more of a beatnik than an artist. Mrs. Loper was small in stature with light brown-blondish hair. They were always pleasant, but clearly preoccupied with whatever art project was at hand. They lived in a simple cinder block rancher with a small garden in the back of the property enclosed with a cinder block fence, which offered some protection from the curious eyes of their neighbors.

The garbage was always full of castaway canvases and frames... product deemed unworthy of the signature of the artist. Bonnie's sister and her new buddy, Dottie, seemed to have great fun digging through this pile of refuge. They built a lot of dollhouses, cars, and anything else their imaginations could come up with. It was their secret stash, and the Lopers seemed to enjoy watching the various projects the girls assembled across the street from their home.

Many of the children in the community took music or voice lessons. During the 1950s and '60s, no education was complete unless you were studying an instrument of some sort. One youngster in the community excelled beyond all others: Ernest Watts Jr., better known as Ernie. This young man played a trumpet like no one else. He practiced all hours of the day and night. Into the wee hours of the morning, you could hear him running scales over and over until you thought you would go mad. The sound of his trumpet bounced around the walls of the homes in the neighborhood with an ebb and flow similar to waves on the ocean. The sounds could lull you to sleep, make you pat your feet, do the boogaloo, or even cry when Ernie made his trumpet wail like a newborn child. Eventually, Mr. Watts would cry uncle, and Ernie had to put the trumpet away. But on most occasions, Ernie's impromptu concerts were a real treat for the neighborhood. Imagine what a surprise it was when upon graduation from Wilmington High, Ernie landed a job on *The Tonight Show* with Johnny Carson's band. Ernest Watts Jr. continued to pursue his dreams and left quite a legacy for others who wanted to move up and out.

The neighborhood also had its own impresario, Mr. Mitchell Thomas. Mr. Thomas produced, directed, and hosted a local dance program for Negro teenagers in the Wilmington community. The Mitch Thomas Show, a talent showcase for local Negro youths, provided a close look at the abilities and interests of students of all economic backgrounds across the city. It was the first show of its type in Wilmington and a groundbreaker for youth and Negro entertainment. Everyone wanted to be on the show. Mr. Thomas was always humble, quiet, and kind, extending a helping hand to as many youths as possible through the show.

Of course, neither of Bonnie's parents was satisfied that their neighbors could suffice as role models for the arts, music, or entertainment, so they regularly exposed them to plays on Broadway, such as Flower Drum Song; the Philadelphia Ballet; Radio City Music Hall; The Philadelphia Philharmonic Orchestra; and many other venues, such as museums, art shows, and world fairs. Both of them were constantly searching for ways to extend their children's understanding of the world and its vast possibilities. Distance and money didn't deter Beily or Richard in their determination to expose them to a bigger, brighter world to come.

One summer, Beily packed the kids up and took them to Boston. Another year, they went to Montreal and got lost in the rural areas of Quebec. Undeterred, Beily told Bonnie she'd have to use her eighth-grade French to help her find the way back to the main highway. Having no choice but to speak what she knew with confidence, Bonnie did just that. Beily was fearless, or at least she made them think she was. She taught: Don't waste your time being afraid. Face the situation down with a smile. Do the best with what you have, and go for it.

Richard taught them to always plan time with your family on a visit to a major city for the best in entertainment. He made sure they got to Radio City for the Christmas and Easter shows, always ending with dinner at The Oyster House or Horn and Hardart. He always took lots of change so they could pick out exactly the menu they wanted, put the coins in the slot, and watch the waiter put the entrée, dessert, or other item in the slot. It was quite a treat to see the "restaurant in a wall" concept and to experience the hustle and bustle of New York City, so unlike sleepy Wilmington. Bonnie's dad had a bit of wanderlust, so he made sure they got to experience all the major sightseeing and tourist sites in Philadelphia, New York, and Washington, D.C., while he wove tales about his war years and dancing in the Savoy and the Cotton Club.

As the oldest child, Bonnie always sat in the front seat of the car next to her parents. She was always the copilot, handing them the change for the turnpike toll, or reading the map, or giving them a sip of water out of the thermos, while Boo and Skip slept in the backseat. In that position, when the radio couldn't pick up the signal or the signal was lost, they talked a lot about current events, their youth, their parents, life in general, and their hopes and dreams for one another. It was the place where Bonnie picked up a lot of family history and wisdom over and over until it stuck in her head and she could repeat the stories like ABC's: Get an education. Get all you can! Serve and trust in the Lord Jesus! Work Hard! Do the very best at whatever you put your mind and hands to. No job is too small not to give it your best. Always be clean. Always be kind. Pray hard and always. You are the oldest; you set the example. Boo and Skip are watching. They will follow you. Be the best you can at whatever you do.

This was the space and time that Bonnie really felt the weight of being the oldest child and her responsibilities at that time and in the future. Just as in the Bible when Elijah cast his cloak to Elisha to pass the anointing from one generation to the next, as the copilot in the car for her parents, a baton of responsibility to maintain the continuity in our story of love, family, and the pursuit of excellence was being passed to Bonnie. Without question or hesitation, she took it and ran. There was no chance to pause or think. It was what you did as a child at that time. It was the circle of life, death, and renewal that was passed from generation to generation. This was Bonnie's little cog in the wheel. Time to press.

"IT'S OVER!"

Shortly after Dr. King's passing, Bonnie was excited to be graduating. She had a great summer job assignment as a lab assistant at the Experimental Station for E. I. duPont de Nemours Inc., which she had secured through the Upward Bound Program. This job would give her the opportunity to save up for her books and sundries at school and, hopefully, get her through the first semester without having to work too many hours. Nothing put a damper on her enthusiasm, not even the constant presence of the National Guard patrolling the streets, bayonets in the air, looking at the neighborhood residents with mean, detached expressions.

Bonnie bounded down the stairs to meet her mom in the living room. She was dressed beautifully in a sheath and heels. After giving Bonnie a big hug and a kiss, Beily said, "This is a big accomplishment, Bonnie. Are you excited?" "Oh, yes, Momma," Bonnie said. "Is water wet? Is seven up? Are grits groceries? Yes, I'm so excited I'm about to pop wide open," she said, giving her a squeeze and a kiss. "Mom, I've got to get going. Butch is supposed to meet you here, and you know he's always late. If he's too late, leave his ticket here, and let Boo and Skip give it to him. Whatever you do, don't be late. This is the most exciting day of my life so far, and I don't want you to miss any of it!" With that said, Bonnie rushed out the door.

Bonnie walked to school, following the same path she had every day for the past three years, carrying her cap and gown. Her classmates gathered in their assigned classrooms, according to where they fell in the alphabet. Two classrooms, for last names beginning with A-L and M-Z, were set aside for girls on one side of the hall. Similarly, two rooms were set aside for the boys on the other side of the hall. They were dressed in their Sunday best with their hair in the latest style. It was a time of hugs and good lucks and good-byes. Many of them were off to college. Others were on their way to Vietnam, having signed up early for a place in their favored branch of service. Some had good jobs waiting. Some were still searching. But they were all on their way into the world as adults, each of them stepping on a path that they had fashioned by commission or omission over the past twelve years, the results sometimes pleasing and sometimes not.

As their teachers lined them up for the last time, there were hugs and smiles and tears. Many of the students had been together as group members since seventh grade or earlier. They had bonded into their own little society, with their own rules and mores. They hadn't been beyond this circle of protection ever. It would be interesting to see how the greater community in this time of flux would respond as they stepped outside of this semi-protected environment into the world. Would their beliefs be honored or dashed to bits? Only time would tell.

To the commencement march, they entered the auditorium. Slowly coming down the center hall, they could see their parents and loved ones in the audience, clapping, smiling, and cheering for them. They broke the formation at the front of the auditorium, one person to the left and one to the right, both heading up the stairs to the risers. Once they had gathered and their audience got to see them all together, they sang their alma mater for the last time. It was a tearful event for some and a hallelujah moment for others.

In the final address to their class, Peter Luce spoke of the challenges of the civil rights movement, the Vietnam War, and the women's movement as some of the great issues they would be expected to grapple with and change during their lifetime. Bonnie was so anxious to get her tassel and celebrate that she hardly heard a word. All she could think of was: *It's over! It's over! Time to move on and out into the world.*

Principal Martin was called to the podium to announce the class valedictorian. This name and the salutatorian's were shrouded in secrecy until the last minute. "The valedictorian of the class of 1968 of Wilmington High School is Bonita Aileen Byrd," Mr. Martin said. For a moment, Bonnie's world was suspended. Everything was moving in slow motion. As the secretary of the Student Council, Bonnie was seated on the front row, and so didn't have far to walk, but her legs felt like lead. She stood up slowly and walked to the podium, where Mr. Martin handed her a specially wrapped box and an envelope. She looked out to see Beily and Butch smiling and clapping for her. She was a little wobbly as she returned to her seat. Mr. Martin began to call out different awards to the class – the highest grades in English, social studies, and so on. That evening, Bonnie was awarded every academic award except in chemistry, and that went to Ernest Talbert Jr. No one could have been more shocked than Bonnie. She studied because she liked to study. Understanding the material of her subjects was reward enough. However, the recognition of her teachers was important to her because it validated all the sacrifices her mom, her nana, and her dad had made for her all her life. The awards served to honor their hard work, their sacrifices, and their guidance. Bonnie was grateful she could begin to show them tangible rewards.

After that, the rest of the evening was a blur. So many friends and classmates congratulated her. Those she didn't get to speak with that night were kind enough to call and express their happiness the next day.

Her only sadness was that her nana and dad were unable to get the evening off to attend the graduation ceremony. Nana made a point to come over the next afternoon. She and Bonnie sat and reviewed the commencement program together. Bonnie explained every award, and Nana took each one out of the box or envelope and held it, turned it over in her hands, and marveled at the accomplishments of her granddaughter.

149

"This is good, Bonnie. This is very good." She leaned forward to take Bonnie's hands into her own. Nana looked deeply into Bonnie's eyes and said: "You see what I am. I'm a cook. You see what your mother is. She's a nurse. And now you know how far you have to go. Understand?" "Yes, Nana, I understand. I have a long way to go to move the family forward." "Uh-huh," she replied. "Now you understand what life is really about. With God's help, you can do it." Bonnie replied, "I'll try my very best, Nana… My very best."

Bonnie spent the rest of her life traveling that long road in an attempt to honor the sacrifices of her dear nana and her parents. Sometimes she'd think she'd accomplished something worthwhile; other times she'd think she'd fallen so short of her own expectations that she was unworthy of the mantle they had passed on to her. For certain, though, the grit, the moxie, the character, and the raw native ability they shared with her have always enabled her to find that place within to pull herself up and push herself forward when all seemed lost and the future seemed so dark and frightening. Their collective light and that of Jesus the Christ continue to shine the path forward, and she knows they will continue until she's with them again. Till then, she's on assignment to pass the lessons forward to their grandchildren and great-grandchildren… to ensure that Addie, Richard, and Beily live forever through these lessons and values, to ensure that their family moves forward, forward, always forward, never retreating, but pressing on to that high mark in Christ Jesus.

Chapter 27

A TRIBUTE TO NANA

Often when they discuss and portray the life of Negroes who were servants to wealthy white families, the picture is sanitized, carefully portraying a symbiotic relationship where the employer and the employee benefited equally.

However, nothing could be further from the truth. From the 1930s through the 1970s, pay was rarely fair or equitable. Most household helpers were not paid with the proper deductions for Social Security, Medicare, or state or federal taxes. Few were paid a decent living wage that afforded them savings for retirement. In fact, one could work her entire life in service to a family and never expect any offer of a retirement plan at all. The best that could be hoped for were the cast-offs – the furniture, clothing, and goods that the employer no longer wanted and offered to the employee for her use. The food that somehow made its way from the employer to the employee's home often was anticipated by the employer and expensed as wages for the employee or pilferage by the employee and written off the employer's taxes as an in-kind expense incurred with household help.

Nana had encountered the full range of employers: the generous and the mean and the hateful. Always respectful and willing to serve her employers to the best of her abilities, Nana prepared meals for hundreds of guests, all with the same level of excellence and attention to detail. Her repertoire of dishes included everything from gourmet pound cake, yeast rolls, and popovers to steak tartare and tomato aspic. No matter what she prepared, she did so in excellence. She was up and in the kitchen by 5 AM and often didn't finish her meals and clean-up until early the next morning. Nana never complained to her employers. She did everything alone from soup to nuts – meal prep, sous chef duties, cooking, and all clean-up. She never had an assistant, unless Beily, Bonnie, Boo, or Skip was at hand. Indeed, Addie Foust was a one-woman wonder, walking quickly across the cork floor of the Rusts' kitchen, swinging her arthritic knees from the hip, replying, "Yes, Colonel" or, "No, Missus" to their inquiries and comments.

A couple of her employers, such as the Rusts, permitted her family to visit Nana on location because they had large estates and the help had a separate section of the house for their own use, complete with bedrooms, a bath, a laundry, and a living room. The dogs always hung out at the servant's quarters; they became familiar with the smells and comings and goings of the hired help's families. Over time, the dogs didn't even bark when Beily and her children drove the three-mile trek from the main highway to the private driveway that connected to the estate. In their own way, these employers were kind and generous. Bonnie was allowed to select a Donald Brooks, silk and linen, designer gown and coat ensemble for her prom at their expense, and they were kind in recognizing her academic achievements in conversation with Nana.

What they didn't do was release Nana on the precious days and times that belong to every family – Christmas, Easter, Sundays for church, birthdays, and evenings. It was her time away from her family that hurt so much. The time that Nana rocked their grandchildren on her lap instead of Bonnie, Boo, or Skip... it was stolen time from the family, snatched in bits and pieces without permission or caring.

The cholly who refused to grant you a mortgage and who cursed you attending a white school was the same cholly whose domestic needs trumped your need for the guidance and wisdom only grandparents can pass down; the warmth, love, and self-acceptance that only nanas can model for you. That was the thing about Cholly – no matter how well you prepared, no matter how cogent the argument, the cholly card always trumped your needs, situation, arguments, and truth... every time; it was that unearned privilege that only white skin can acquire in this wonderful country of ours.

As Bonnie grew older and more aware, she began to understand that the price of her loved one's employment and the perks the employers provided her was the loss of her presence in Bonnie's life. As she approached high school, she can remember saying that there was something unfair about Nana's employment situation, and Dr. King was marching about it. Bonnie told her Dr. King said change was coming, and she added, "Nana, when the change comes, I'm gonna take you home, and we will cook all the cakes and pies we want. We will have tea parties all day every day." Nana would just smile and say, "Ahkapushnik!" That was her way of saying, "Be quiet and grateful."

Bonnie resented sharing Nana with the employers' grandchildren and hated seeing photographs of her posing with little Ms. So-and-So and Little Mr. So-and-So. Nana loved these kids, but when her time at the job ended, her employers had no problem dumping her like so much trash without even an afterthought.

Then, like a thief in the night, her cancer returned. Beily received a call early one morning asking her to please come pick up her mother. She was moaning and couldn't get up to work properly anymore. So Beily drove out to Chateau Country faster than the legal limit, packed up Nana, and brought her home. She had been preparing the house for Nana's retirement years earlier, converting the garage into a bedroom with an en suite bath. The next morning, Butch – now Bonnie's husband, Alton – and Bonnie received a call to please come help Beily take Nana to the hospital, as she was in terrible pain. They rushed to 301. Bonnie had never seen Nana grimace or writhe in pain. Tears fell from Bonnie's eyes at the sight. Her heroine, her leader was in deep trouble, and she didn't know what to do to help. Beily's face was so pinched and fearful. She couldn't be really sick. Nana was just sixty-five years old. She was finally retired, and there were still tea parties to hold and lessons to learn. "Dear Father, hold onto my nana. I can't imagine a world without her," Bonnie prayed.

Later that morning, Beily called Bonnie at work to advise her that Nana had cancer. In 1974, this was a death sentence. They had six weeks or less with her, as she was very ill. The focus became doing everything they could to secure Nana's comfort. For the first time in Bonnie's life, she could see her mom was really shaken to the core. Bonnie knew she had to step up her input and contribution. The first task at hand was to drop by the hospital to check on things there. When she looked in the room, she was struck by how thin her nana was in the bed. She was obviously in pain. *Where in the Sam Hill was the nurse?* Bonnie wondered. As she looked around, it was obvious that the room was not up to par. It definitely was not as clean as she'd like, and the amenities due her queen were not in place.

Bonnie embraced her mom. "You okay?" Bonnie asked, knowing that she wasn't, but hoping her embrace would help her keep it together. Beily looked up at Bonnie with red-rimmed eyes. "Momma, take a break. There are some things I can do here," Bonnie insisted. "You sure?" Beily asked, almost as though she needed permission. "Yes, Momma, I can do this. Take a break. Let me do the honors," Bonnie said. Bonnie kissed her cheek and sent her off. "Don't come back for a while. I'm in no hurry."

Bonnie leaned over Nana, smoothing her thick hair back from her face. She was feverish and pale, her complexion so unlike what Bonnie was accustomed to seeing. Bonnie found a small pail in her dresser and some washcloths in the bathroom. She made the water tepid, as Beily had taught her years ago. She tested a drop on the inside of her wrist to make sure it wasn't too hot, wrung out the cloth till it was nearly dry, and gently patted the skin around Nana's face, wiping the sweat from her brow and praying somehow she could pat the cancer away with it. *Bonnie's here, Nana. I'll do my best to do it right*, Bonnie thought.

Finally, a nurse appeared. Bonnie introduced herself and asked when Nana would be given something for the pain and when the doctor would be coming. Neither response was satisfactory. "Could you please administer something to get the pain under control? If you are unable to do so, please put me in immediate contact with someone who can make the decision." Clearly, these folks were not used to a twenty-something-year-old black woman speaking so directly and with an in-charge attitude. Maybe that's what an education from Brown University had bought her. Whatever it was, the nurse picked up from the inflection in her voice she wasn't to be trifled with. Nana got a shot of morphine, and Bonnie thanked God as she watched Nana's body relax and grateful oblivion seep into her consciousness.

Bonnie's boss at New Castle County, Jim Gilliam Sr., was on the board of directors for the hospital. She contacted him at home, advising him of her grandmother's illness and her dissatisfaction with the medical services and cleanliness of Nana's room. He placed a call to the head of the board, and before Beily had returned, Nana had been relocated to a clean, sunny room with nice appointments, and the doctor had showed up full of concern. After introductions, Bonnie let him know politely who his patient was and that while he hadn't had the pleasure of knowing her, she was one of the greatest people who had ever lived... and that Bonnie expected her to be treated as such. He looked at Bonnie quite curiously as she assured him that she had the ear of the head of the board of the hospital and that while she would be loath to say anything derogatory about his care being neglectful, she wasn't above doing anything necessary to ensure the best quality of care possible for her nana, regardless of the expense. Bonnie closed by letting him know that her nana's former employers were among the largest donors to the hospital, and if necessary, she would not hesitate to contact them.

The doctor didn't know that Nana's former employer cared less than a fig about Bonnie's sweetie, but she was so very tired of Cholly. Bonnie was determined that nothing, not even racist perceptions of her grandmother, would undermine the ability for her to secure the best quality care and provisions for Nana. It was the least Bonnie could do for the pillar of her existence. Bonnie was shaken. Her world was permanently changed. She was a real adult now, and she wasn't sure how to measure victory in this situation. She began to take each day as a battle, watching Nana's strength drain away, guiding Beily through the legal mess of getting the house and assets in her name to avoid inheritance taxes.

One quiet evening, the angels came and welcomed her nana to her new home. The family members all cried and embraced, unable to fully comprehend the experience of life without their dear, sweet Addie, the foundation of their family, the strength of their lineage.

The funeral was held at St. Matthew's, and an interim pastor conducted the worst service Bonnie had ever seen at the church. Surely, he had none of the polish or love that Fathers Wilson and Casson had extended to their family. He didn't even know Nana's name and had to be prompted by Beily during the service. It left a bitter taste in their mouths and led to their leaving St. Matthew's for quite a while.

Our family buried Nana at Riverside Cemetery, close to the pine trees that were reminiscent of those on the homestead in Winston Salem, North Carolina, where she was born. To this day, I miss her terribly. Every time I set the table, or attempt to replicate her yeast rolls, I return to a three year old, standing in the kitchen at 301 waiting to hear her, "Hello, sweet baby!" Her chair sits in my living room as a tribute to her strength and love. When things get crazy and I need the wisdom of the sages, I sit in her chair and pray to God for wisdom and guidance. A calm always comes over me. Like a fresh breeze, I hear Nana's voice and see her face, as clearly as when

I'd sneak into her bed at my childhood bedroom. My nana is always alive in me through her love for me. As I pass it forward to my sons, it lives forever.

Chapter 28

"THANK YOU, DADDY"

It is often said that children do not come with instructions in their pants. This rationale is used to explain why it is often difficult for parents to decipher what a child needs to thrive and develop properly. Much the same could be said from the child's perspective when somehow something doesn't quite click in the parent child relationship. The child gropes about trying to put the relationship together, feeling strained and labored in the attempt to bring a satisfactory response but somehow always falling short of the child's desired response. Such was the case between my dad and I. I always felt, somehow, something was lacking in me. Something that failed to elicit a special chuckle or smile. Oddly, Dad and I had a lot in common. He had been the eldest son, responsible for helping his parents to negotiate a new life in Delaware. Similarly, I was the eldest child, responsible for helping my mother to negotiate life as a single parent and raise a sister and brother. I assumed this role independent of guidance from my mother. Rather it was a sense of responsibility that was "wired in" so to speak, by birth order, by innate responses to your surroundings, the cues I picked up, acted upon, or not. Daddy and I struggled to negotiate a father-daughter divide we found ourselves in. Both of us trying to love my mom and siblings and support one another while our lives evolved as father and daughter.

The roughest times were when the support check was late. I was the one who had to ask Dad for the forty-five dollar check. Fifteen dollars a month per child was what the court awarded my mom. It was a critical amount of money in our household. It tended to create a lot of angst and animosity between us. Later listening to my dad's ranting during our weekly visits about how he could say one word and the judge would return us all to his household even after the divorce was enough to make my stomach turn for hours after I'd returned home to 301.

But Dad persisted in being a parent as best he knew how, despite the impediments and stigma of divorce. Every Saturday morning at 9 AM sharp you could count on Dad being parked outside 301 at the curb in his shiny, black Ford Thunderbird ready to spend the day with his three kids. Come rain, snow, sleet, hail Dad was there. Waiting. Without expectation. Never complaining about my occasional no shows. Skip was his faithful compadre and because of that the two of them reaped an unbelievably close relationship and mutual respect. He taught Richard Lee (Skip) how to be a man... How to face adversity and overcome it. He challenged Skip; Treated him to rewards – several Chevy Stingrays – for his academic success; Supported his education from undergrad through dental school and two post graduate dental degrees. Mom and I were eternally grateful to him for that support and the payoff for that personal investment continues to reap dividends through his grandchildren.

Daddy showed me agape love without ever saying, "I love you." He bought me tailor made suits and a ruby ring for my birthday. He drove 16 hours round trip to be with me for Parent's weekend at Brown my freshman year which was a godsend. I was so lonesome for home I couldn't see straight. Five years later he bought my nontraditional wedding dress, eschewing a traditional white dress for a bright African print to match my "I'm black and I'm proud" big, round Afro. Daddy didn't attend my wedding, though. He was too afraid of what mom's reaction to his presence might be. He had grown weary of the rejection, and it hurt him to see her move physically as far away from him as she could get. That was when I realized that my daddy did love my momma. His quiet, complacent forbearance and deference toward her needs at the expense of his own indicated a love and respect one rarely, if ever, witnesses in the "in your face" response to rejection one sees so often in todays world.

Daddy just didn't know the love story she needed him to follow to live with her. That was when I began to realize how much we had all lost… what could have been… what grief both of my parents had lived with – suffered through – after the marriage had ended… why my Dad had fought so hard to maintain the relationship he had with his family.

The divide between my parents was great as they reached for each other through each other's childhood experiences. My Dad saw the role of husband as that of a protector, provider, controller – a traditional, agrarian role model for that century, time, and means. That role was tested and tempered by the confines, prejudices and fears of a Negro man in the 1940's and 50's. My Momma's perspective was as a Negro employee in an upper class white household devoid of any male figure at all and the frequently precarious position of a child who was constantly threatened with abandonment issues due to the vicissitudes of race, poverty, and the poor health of her mother and father. As household help, Momma was never really viewed by the Apple sisters as a human being, having equal value or merit. I'm sure my momma's expectations for marriage were skewed by this white picture of family relationships, in contrast to the reality of marital relationships among Negroes in the 1950's. Momma used to say that when a Negro is raised by a white their outlook is always a bit different in outlook. That difference in perspective results from living on the cusp of two different, often diametrically opposed, cultures. The inability of either of my parents to reach across these divides surely impacted their ability to pull their marriage together.

But Momma and Daddy did their best to reach through the smoke and mirrors and confusion to bond across the things that divided them. Often there were glimpses of what they could fulfill together. Clearly they had the potential to be leaders in their community of

Claymont. They once threw a Halloween party for all of the kids who lived on Hickman Row in the basement of their home. The party featured costumes and apple bobbing, and all kinds of games and other fun and good eats. They were the first and only middle class couple in the area that cared enough to live and lead where they had set down roots. They had no idea how threatening a concept this was to together Negro who lived in nearby Wilmington, nor how much jealousy their very youth, beauty, and achievements, and potential created among others far less able.

When trouble struck their relationship there was no help to be had. They had no real friends to confide in because they were both loners. They had no agency or relationship experts to whom they could turn for guidance. They had no spiritual leaders to offer guidance and point the way to healing. There was no bridge between them to walk across, or love across. Daddy and Momma stood at the edge of their desolateness, looking helplessly at each other, until the weight of the situation was too much to bear. So they made the conscious choice to hold onto their three children and to mold the three of us into a bridge that would hold them and sustain the five of us through the madness of divorce and its aftermath and into eternity as a family.

And it was so.

Despite what the experts might say, I can tell you as the child of divorced parents I never got over the split up of my parents. I always wanted my parents reunited, or at the very least, I wanted the time I'd lost living apart from my Dad. And God made a way to recoup what was lost.

Many years later I had to become a stay-at-home mom due to a chronic illness my son was experiencing. It also afforded me the time to focus on my Dad's care because he was beginning to evince signs of Alzheimer's disease and dementia. My cousin Henry (June) Byrd Jr., at Richard Lee's request, had moved in with my Dad as a companion and nurse, and made sure Dad had clean clothes, watched television, and got around in the house safely. Henry did all of this while working a full time job and taking care of his own failing health. Together we managed to get Dad into an adult day care program specializing in Alzheimer's clients. Later when his needs exceeded what could be addressed in a home environment we moved Dad to a nursing home close by. In some small way I hoped that this period of caring for my father compensated for all I wished I could have done to honor this great man I was privileged to call my father. I was so sorry for all of the misunderstandings that stood between us these many years. I hoped every time I gently held his frail body as I put him in the car or his wheelchair, it conveyed how much I loved my Daddy.

One fall day, in 2007, I came home from church to find a note from my sister, Beily, asking me to call her as soon as possible. Dad had passed away. When I saw my daddy's body I was struck by how small and frail he appeared. The life force of God makes the earthen vessel so much more than its substance really is. This is never more apparent than in death. What this great man of character had accomplished during his life could only have been done in the presence and under the anointing of a loving God.

Daddy had accomplished so much that he did not receive credit for. He transitioned his family from Havana Plantation to Delaware. He cared for his parents all of their lives. He built homes for his parents and his family. He loved and supported his wife and children his entire life. He didn't walk away from his family even after a divorce. He taught his daughters their worth and how a man should treat them. He adored his seven grandchildren. He left a legacy of education, hard work and an indomitable spirit and a love for God that would propel his family forward in faith, commitment and sacrifice. There was nothing left for him to do or to give us. He gave it all.

Yes, my Daddy was there. Present and accounted for. I thank God for my Dad because I would not be who I am but for Richard Airee D. Byrd. As my brother Richard said, Momma was like a comet; if you missed her you missed a never again phenom. But Daddy was the sun. He was the constant, silent, stabilizing force quietly operating from a distance. Momma would not have shone as brightly as she did had it not been for the light she reflected from Daddy. I can see it now that I'm grown.

I loved my Daddy very much and I wished I'd told him more often while he was here. It took me sixty years to figure out that that my world had three pillars of support: Nana, Momma, and Daddy. Yes his guidance, support and love were essential for me to thrive and survive. I know that now. So, thank you Daddy. Thank you for everything!

Chapter 29

MOMMA: MY HEROINE/MY FRIEND

Ilearned quite early that the heroes/heroines in my life lived under the same roof that I did. Unlike the culture we live in today during the post World War II era you were taught the men and women who got up every day to work in the home or outside of it to ensure you had food to eat, clothes on your back, a roof over your head, these were the people worthy of celebration and honor. You knew your life and wellbeing were completely dependent upon their willingness to sacrifice so that you could enjoy the wonderful life you were living – free from obligation or worry. I knew my momma was my heroine and I had no problem expressing it to her or anyone who cared to listen.

My earliest recollection of my mother and our relationship goes back to when I was about two years old. Momma was on the way to the hospital to give birth to my sister. She was in the front passenger seat moaning. I was in the rear seat of the car troubled by her obvious pain and discomfort. "Mommy does your tummy hurt? Bonnie rub," I remember saying. Ours was a unique relationship: mother and daughter, but also sister and sister, and, most of all, deeply loving, faithful friends, forever.

Watching her get ready for work was a time of intimacy for me. I'd lie at the end of her bed facing her dresser. Seated with her back toward me, her reflection in the mirror that rose from waist high, midway to the ceiling I'd observe her comb her hair and apply her make up. First she did her hair. Each half of her pompadour was angled just so with the heel of her hand and fingers. Then, ever so carefully she placed the bobby pin at the end of the lock, twisted into a pin curl. She repeated this series of actions on the other half of the pompadour. She'd reach to the back of her head and gather her hair into a low ponytail that she twirled around on one finger to form a bun. Then her make up: moisturizer, powder patted on sparingly over her nose and cheeks, carefully arching the brows, darkening the beauty mark at the side of her mouth and outlining her full lips in a soft red Max Factor lipstick which she blotted with a tissue she had folded and placed on the left side of the dresser. Finally, the most important aspect of her dressing routine: placing the starched, white nursing cap on her head and pinning her Provident Hospital pin over her heart. A little hand lotion, a dab of perfume, a quick glance at her white nursing shoes and Momma was ready for her students at the Drew/Pyle Elementary School.

I was in awe of my momma. She'd flash her mega watt smile at me and kiss me on the cheek before she left the house for work. I never wiped the red kiss mark off my face. Ever. It was a reminder that she loved me and I treasured that visible sign of her love.

Momma was so much more than a pretty face, though. She was extremely well read. She introduced me to Pushkin, Baudelaire, Balzac, Baldwin and LeRoi Jones aka Amire Baraka. She loved music of every type classical, jazz, and R&B. Nobody loved James Brown more than my mom. Nobody. She was an artist and a needlewoman crafting everything from clothing to decoupage purses. She shared her love of reading with me and encouraged me to read everything that would reflect positively on the mirror of the soul. Every morning that she rose you would find her at 5 AM reading her red bible at the kitchen table as the coffee pot perked away. She started every day with the guidance and presence of the Lord before her. His was the hand she held to start her day and throughout. It is a memory I call upon often when life is challenging for me.

Beily Paige was a woman of character with standards and principles that she lived by. She chose not to date or pursue a relationship until all three of her children had left home. (My Dad never let us see him with another woman until we were all in our twenties with families of our own either.) Even when those relationships disappointed, Momma never complained or appeared desolate or despondent. Instead, she redirected her energies. She never allowed herself the luxury of boredom or self-pity. She never became a couch potato or a television addict. She never believed in idleness, either mental or physical.

Momma loved her people. She believed it was important to know who you were and whose you were. That began with a relationship with the Lord but it expanded into a thorough understanding of African American History. When I was in the second grade she gave me her Negro History book, signed by Langston Hughes, to take to school for show and tell. Momma made sure her children knew what role our people spent in building this country and the cultural contributions we made from Benjamin Banneker to the Fisk Jubilee Singers and Leontyne Price. She made sure we did the same for our children. Momma understood that until we were secure in our blackness we could not walk in complete confidence as we progressed through life. She made sure we had a sound racial foundation so that we need never feel intimidated by the "you come from slaves" mantra all African American children are hit with when you enter school and become exposed to the indoctrination of the "you are less than" lie. These were hard won lessons from a ba'faced injun gal who had managed to rise above the bunk to become the first African American public health nurse in Delaware. I was a very fortunate person to have been groomed by such a forward thinking woman. Momma believed children were like clay. They had to be molded and I was molded by the best.

Through life's challenges and blessings Momma aged gracefully. She never wrinkled or lost her hair or beauty to the bitter end. Having taught me how to live life to the fullest, Momma showed me how to let life go gracefully in its proper time. Several strokes eventually impaired her ability to speak and the situation was further complicated by an accompanying dementia. Communication became somewhat difficult. It was difficult to see my momma like this. We had had so many wonderful talks. Interacting with someone suffering from dementia is like reaching through the ethers to grasp a moment of clarity only to watch it disappear before it has actually manifested. You get glimpses of your loved one, as you knew them, until gradually they are no more. You get a quick smile of recognition, a nod, the tilt of the head, and then they're gone. Faded away until the next all too brief visitation. I pledged that my momma had been so gracious to walk me through life from birth through sixty that the very least I could do was to walk her home to the Lord and place her hand in His. It was an honor, a pleasure and humbling to return all she had invested in me through this small act.

It was through persistence, consistency, sacrifice, and pain – yes, real pain – that Momma moved her three children and seven grandchildren forward physically, mentally, emotionally, and spiritually. Addie Foust was the foundation and pillar number one; Richard Airee D. Byrd was the silent, unheralded ever-present strength and pillar number two; but Beily Paige Foust Byrd, Momma, was the universal joint sending life and power into every part of the family, both immediate and extended, as pillar number three. These three wonderful, extraordinary individuals provided the platform from which my sister, brother and I were able to achieve and fly. My Momma's back, though, was the bridge across which we walked from our family's southern roots in Havana and Winston Salem into our positions as lawyer, professional cellist, and orthodontist. It would have never happened without Beily – my nana's Ginger. She was the essential element.

In closing, Momma, your decedents press on. Just as you taught us and your grandchildren to press onward and upward, the Williams, the Streets and the Byrds press as businessmen, dentists, lawyers, statesmen, and musicians… and we will keep coming, keep moving forward, always in honor of your legacy.

God bless you, sweet Momma. I love you now and always.

CPSIA information can be obtained
at www.ICGtesting.com
Printed in the USA
FFOW01n1902291215
19700FF